SYDNEY 2000

The Games of the XXVII Olympiad
The Official Souvenir Book

Sydney 2000

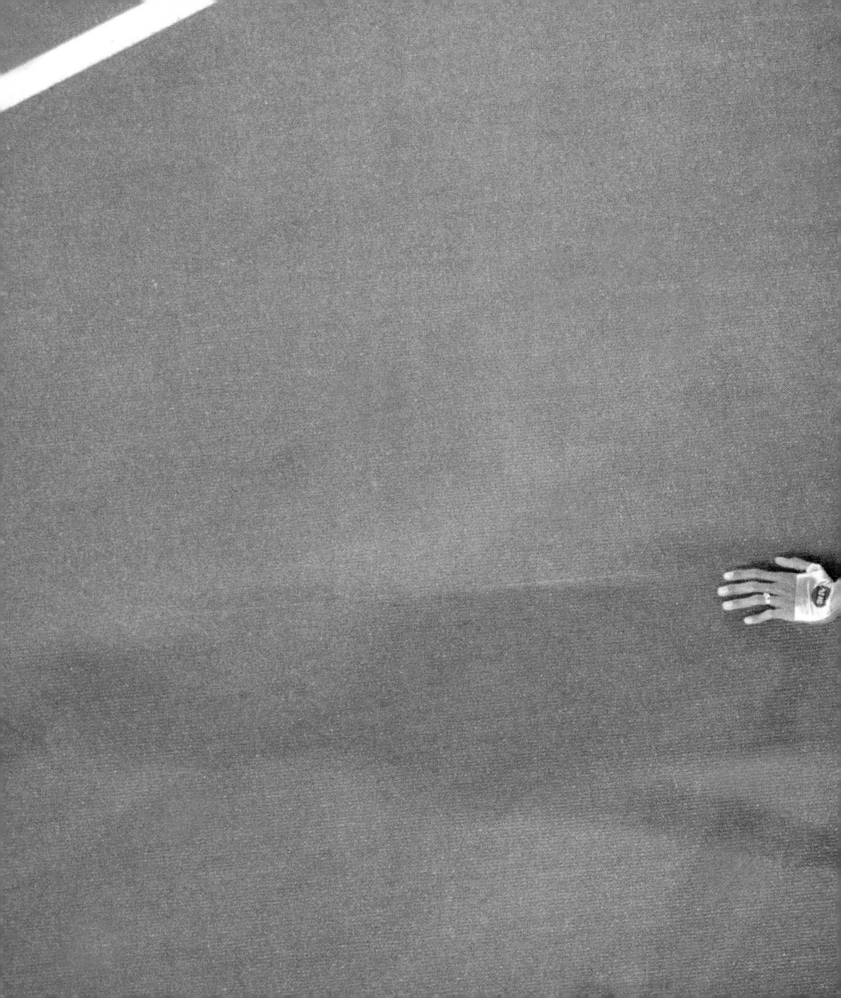

Publisher
Nick Trompf

Managing Editor
James Weston

Editor
Michelle Brown

Art Director
Andrew Hutchison

Designers
Annthea Hick
Miriam Rudolph

Picture Editor
Terry Phelan

Copy Editor
Tony Fawcett

Results
Michelle Ainley

Marketing Manager
Rik Schnabel

Administrator
Jenine Tinker

Quality Control/Imaging Manager
Graham Patrick

Editorial Production Manager
Michael Brown

Print Manager
John Batten

Production Co-ordinator
Cathy Murray

Color Separations
HWT Imaging

Printing
PMP Print

Binding
Griffin Press

Book industry distribution
Hardie Grant

Corporate sales
Edgar P Spallek and Karin M Adolf

TM © SOCOG 1998
© IOC/Olympic Museum Collection

Published by
 News Custom Publishing,
a division of the Herald and Weekly
Times Ltd,
ACN 004 113 937, HWT Tower,
40 City Road, Southbank, VIC 3006.

Order your personal copy of photographs within
this book – visit www.newsphotos.com.au
or freecall 1300 301 705 (some exceptions apply).

Photography

Daily Telegraph
Marco Del Grande, Brett Costello, Mark Evans,
Phil Hillyard, John Feder, Pip Blackwood,
Jeff Darmanin, Roy Haverkamp, Jim Trfyllis,
Glen Dickerson, Rob McKell, Nathan Edwards,
Bob Barker, Brad Newman, Jeff Herbert,
Tara Johns, Jason Busch, Gregg Porteous.

Sunday Telegraph
Michael Perini, Kristy Miller, Simon Cocksedge.

Herald Sun
Craig Borrow, Michael Dodge, Colleen Petch,
George Salpigtidis, Jay Town, Peter Ward,
Simon Dallinger, Fiona Hamilton, Mike Keating,
David Caird.

Sunday Herald Sun
Darren Tindale, Karen Dodd.

The Australian
Graham Crouch, Brett Faulkner, Glen Campbell,
Patrick Hamilton, Colin Murty, Mark Williams,
Renee Nowytager, Alan Pryke, Lindsay Moller,
Bob Finlayson, Ross Swanborough.

Brisbane Courier-Mail
Bruce Long, David Kapernick, Anthony Weate,
Mark Cranitch, Nathan Richter.

Hobart Mercury
Leigh Winburn, Tony Palmer, Kim Eiszele.

The Advertiser
Leon Mead, Sarah Reed, Darren Seiler.

Sunday Mail
Mark Brake

Sunday Times
Jackson Findell

Gold Coast Bulletin
Glenn Hampson

Townsville Bulletin
Scott Chisholm

Northern Territory News
Rohan Kelly

Cumberland Newspapers
Peter Clarke, Daniel Griffiths.

Reuters
Sport. The Library
Allsport

You have in your hands the official commemorative book of the Games of the XXVII Olympiad, the first Games of the new millennium, which were held in Sydney, New South Wales, Australia, from 15 September to 1 October 2000.

This book, published by the Organising Committee in cooperation with the International Olympic Committee, relates in detail and with superb illustrations the greatest and most unforgettable moments of Sydney 2000.

There is no doubt that all those who experienced the Games of the XXVII Olympiad, either in Australia or through the audiovisual coverage provided around the world, will find all their happy memories featured in this commemorative work.

Australia, a sporting country par excellence, has met every challenge to ensure the success of these Games dedicated to the athletes, of which the Cultural Olympiad and Opening and Closing Ceremonies have been among the highlights.

On behalf of the Olympic Movement, I would like to take this opportunity to pay tribute and express our gratitude to the people of Australia, the Federal Government, the state of New South Wales, the city of Sydney, the National Olympic Committee, the Organising Committee of the Games of the XXVII Olympiad and the volunteers, for their hospitality and their contribution to the development of sport and the Olympic Ideal.

My sincere thanks also to the athletes, the 28 International Federations and the National Olympic Committees for their active participation, and to our economic partners and the media for their support, as well as to the spectators for their sporting spirit.

The Games of the Olympiad are the biggest gathering of the youth of the world, one of a kind. In a society confronted with social, political, religious and ethnic conflicts, whose victims are often children, the youth and women, sport and the Olympic Ideal provide hope, and the sports field remains the best place for peaceful confrontation.

Sport is a school of human values which we frequent when we are young and need to make further use of as a means of preventative education, in order to face the scourges which poison our society. Investing in education and youth is an investment in the future.

I personally believe that in this new millennium, sport, which is now a social phenomenon, will occupy an ever greater place in the daily lives of humankind.

JUAN ANTONIO SAMARANCH

Marqués de Samaranch
President of the International Olympic Committee

CONTENTS

WORDS | JOHN HAMILTON

THE OLYMPIC CITY

Seven years in the making, the Sydney 2000 Olympic Games were a triumph for the host city and the nation. Variously dubbed the Athletes' Games, the Ultimate Games and the Happy Games, Sydney 2000 is indelibly etched into the memories of 19 million Australians and thousands of international visitors.

Fatso the wombat, national colors, pins — they were all part of the color of Sydney. The harbor city put on its best face to the world, whether at Sydney Olympic Park (above right) or in the final, breathtaking fireworks display (opening spread).

It began with an unknown, tiny 13-year-old girl dabbing zinc cream on her nose, spreading a beach towel in front of 112,524 people and launching a dream that lasted for 17 extraordinary days. A few minutes into the dream and every parent's heart froze. The tiny girl in pink was breaststroking high above Stadium Australia, high above a vast undersea world of giant jellyfish, sea monsters and Great Barrier Reef tropical fish.

The little girl had been holding the hand of an Aboriginal dancer. He was leading her on into the Dreamtime, then exploring the history of the nation. The music of chanting Central Desert women and the throbbing of Torres Strait kundu drums. Visions of bushfires and wildflowers, Ned Kellys and water tanks, fire belching windmills, tap dancing country folk and new arrivals pouring in from many nations, uniting as one. Then the dream developed further, deeper. A slim woman, instantly recognisable, stood in a circle of fire.

Cathy Freeman, dressed in a bodysuit of silvery white, held a flaming torch aloft, a spirit of Australia surrounded by the elements of fire and water thundering behind her in a giant waterfall, signalling what was to come. A symbol of reconciliation, a country together at one purpose. She lit the cauldron. There was a quivering, heart-stopping moment. A small lurch and then it rose upwards as a celestial choir soared with it. The Games of the XXVII Olympiad had begun.

Like all dreams it soon became a kaleidoscope of disconnected images. And it became images of astonishing reality, of sharp clarity — the best athletes in the world performing and the world itself meeting together in Sydney — before fading into a dream again. The dream ended when the little girl, now famous and known to all the world as Nikki Webster, stood on a platform high above the Olympic stadium in the shadow of the giant cauldron where the flame was slowly dying.

The wind was blowing strongly and her white robe floated behind her. She looked like a tiny fairy flying as she sang: "I can't believe the end has come with friendships just begun ... where nations joined to be a better world.

"So let's reach up to the stars ..."

And then a RAAF F-111 fighter bomber thundered overhead belching orange fire from its after-burners. Fireworks exploding in a river of lightning down to the Sydney Harbour Bridge. The Olympic rings themselves exploding outwards.

It was the flaming signal to start the mother of all parties, of celebrations. The dreamlike images that will linger to always be remembered.

It was a party with Kylie Minogue on a giant maroon, yellow and blue thong towed by lifesavers; Greg Norman teeing off from a giant silver shark; Paul Hogan on top of a giant Crocodile Dundee hat, cracking a stockwhip over prawns on bicycles; water buffalo on scooters; rollerblading crocs; frill-necked lizards on unicycles. But above all, the 11,000 athletes from 199 competing nations. Mingled all together regardless of nation or race, religion or creed. Laughing, dancing, singing together. United in peace and joy. The realisation of a suggestion once made by a Melbourne schoolboy, John Wing, back in 1956. At the closing of an Olympic Games there should be no barriers.

Juan Antonio Samaranch had declared this 27th Olympiad to be the best Games ever. Sydney had made it after all.

The Games had been seven years in the making and planning but, often, we thought they would be the Disastrous Games. Only a year ago, the credibility of the organising committee, SOCOG, was in tatters. There was a ticketing fiasco, budget blowouts and a chief executive tendering his resignation. Doomsayers predicted Sydney airport would not handle the traffic, that the road traffic would be at gridlock and the trains would run off the rails. But they didn't. It all worked.

And just in the same way the nation rallies when handling a disaster like a bushfire. Australia rallied again to make sure ... bloody sure ... there would be no disaster. The Games would work.

SOCOG sold a record 92.7 per cent of the 5.7 million tickets allocated with a value of $780 million. Sydney hosted 362,000 domestic and 110,000 international visitors for the Games and a further 1.6 million have been projected to visit Australia as a result of the global television exposure over the next four years, injecting an estimated $6 billion into the tourism industry.

The global television audience for the Games was estimated to be 4 billion. In Australia alone, more than 10 million watched the opening and closing

This page: Beachgoers at Bondi had "free tickets" to watch the USA team practice. The beach was jam packed with fans as was Circular Quay, and the Homebush train station. But keeping everyone smiling throughout were the 47,000 volunteers.

Opposite page: The crowds who trekked to Sydney Olympic Park each day dealt with the crush and the heat, many choosing to dress up for the occasion.

ceremonies and 8,787,000 saw Cathy Freeman's 400m final. Sydney was swamped with 17,000 media from throughout the world.

Forty-seven thousand volunteers came to town, the ever-smiling, ever-courteous, unsung heroes. They were university students and senior citizens. They were school bus drivers from places as faraway as Kyneton and Gilgandra. They put on uniforms of loud cheery blue shirts and white bowls club hats and they just hopped in and did the job that bowled the world over.

"The Sydney Games, with all their uplifting camaraderie, their volunteer altruism and their inspirational struggles, have begun the process of dragging the Olympic Games out of their death spiral and nudging them back towards the pinnacle of world sport," said The Times of London.

"Australia's passion for sport, it is widely agreed, produced the best organised and best spirited Games since the start of the modern era in 1896," said the *Independent*.

"More than anything, these Games restored a common touch and sense of fun to an Olympic movement viewed by many to have been made inaccessible by an aloof, arrogant leadership," wrote the *New York Times*.

Michael Johnson, the great American 400m gold medallist, who ran with golden shoes and a back like an ironing board, had dubbed the whole pageant the Happy Games. And they were.

They had a warmth to them, a glow of goodwill to all mankind that, like the fumes of old cognac, enveloped people along with the Australian sunshine. The sun that never stopped shining, save for an odd thunderstorm that cleared the air of the dust raised by the feet of 400,000 people who, each day, made their way to Sydney Olympic Park.

People on trains and buses were smiling and talking to each other as they made their way to and from the venues. And there were many more places to go than Homebush to see the action. From watching the boats slicing Sydney Harbour, to experiencing the weightlifters hefting barbells at the Convention Centre, to sitting in the bleachers at Bondi watching beach volleyball or travelling way out west to see horses jumping, shooters shooting, kayak paddlers paddling, all Sydney was constantly on the move.

Australian patriots wore their hearts on their sleeve or wherever else it suited them. There were green and gold wigs and green and gold tinsel head dresses, green and gold shirts and shorts and dresses. And the flag, worn as a cloak by spectators or competitors alike.

Above: Thousands had their picture taken so they looked like they were holding the Olympic cauldron, including staunch Australian fan, Sydney's Greg Heaney.

Opposite page, top: Dutch superstar Inge de Bruijn let her hair down and went crowd-surfing at post-Games celebrations.

Opposite page, bottom: Sailor Sara Wright was all packed up and ready to go home to Bermuda.

"Aussie Aussie Aussie Oi Oi Oi!" became a national mantra, even chanted at the closing ceremony by Samaranch and the crowd. And never has the national anthem been sung more often or with greater feeling — with everybody knowing the words.

The fans poured into the Olympic sites day after day; they lined up for trains, for hours at a time, always good-humored.

Visitors from overseas also wore their flags on their heart. One much-photographed Japanese gentleman wore a ceremonial kimono, the crossed flags of Japan and Australia in his straw hat, and a sign round his chest reading "your smile is my gold medal".

Every sport had a packed audience, even sports many fans perhaps had never seen before. Every athlete, every sport was cheered.

A whole carriage sang Waltzing Matilda together at the news the Hockeyroos had won gold again. And on a shuttle bus late at night a driver from the Wimmera talked to the athlete from the prairies of Canada. They compared the price of combine harvesters, then exchanged names and addresses, friends for forever.

These were also the Athletes' Games, with records tumbling like a house of cards. Australia had come fourth in the medal tally with 16 gold, 25 silver, 17 bronze, the best result since 1956.

And they were the Women's Games.

Many and varied were the triumphs to celebrate the 100th anniversary of women first participating in the Olympic Games. The images flash like a slide show — Naoko Takahashi's little smile of surprise when she won the marathon for Japan; Inge de Bruijn, the Dutch swimmer jumping with excitement like a little girl at her birthday surprise after each of her three gold medals; Marion Jones wrapping herself in her flag after running like a gazelle. The icy coolness, the tears of frustration, the triumphant, withering gaze of Russia's pin-up gymnast Svetlana Khorkina as she recovered from falling from the uneven bars on the first night of competition, winning gold on them the next.

Images of golden triumph for Australia's women. The Hockeyroos united, waving their bouquets of

This page: At the end of it all, the fans went home to rest and the international athletes found wherever they could to recover before catching their flights. The crush at Sydney Airport was incredible. Staff processed more passengers in four hours than it would handle on its busiest day.

Opposite page: For the Australian team the parties just kept coming. A ticker-tape parade through the city streets attracted huge crowds and the athletes were more than happy to mingle with the fans – especially for the ever popular Cathy Freeman and pole vault silver medallist Tatiana Gregorieva.

wildflowers; the water polo team wide-armed with happiness; Natalie Cook and Kerri Pottharst clutching the sand, prostrate after winning gold at beach volleyball; the great, wide grin of Lauren Burns as she realised she had suddenly become famous. And Susie O'Neill's look of wide-eyed surprise, then contentment, when she won the 200m freestyle. The look of brave disappointment when she was pipped to win only — only! — silver in her pet butterfly event.

There are many more, of course. Tatiana Grigorieva, the golden pole vaulter winning silver for her new country as Cathy Freeman prepared for glory at the other end of the stadium.

But then an image of disaster. Poor Jane Saville, the Australian walker. The pain, the incredulity, the despair, the pitiful helplessness of a nation watching as the man with the red marker stepped forward from the shadows at the entrance to the main stadium. She was disqualfied a few hundred paces short of winning gold.

There are the images of the men too, perhaps above all, Ian Thorpe, Big Foot himself. His size 17s operating like gas turbine engines to propel him to victory. Thorpe and Hackett, Perkins and Klim, and all the others — a gold and silver-winning frenzy of excitement.

There was Australia's own Robin Hood, Simon Fairweather, arrows thudding home in the bullseye to win gold. The quiet equestrian achievers led by the immaculate Andrew Hoy.

The bad boy of athletics, chain-smoking Jai Taurima, leaping long to win silver. Laconic Michael Diamond shooting those little orange frisbees to win gold. But then the look of dismay on Russell Mark's face when he made one mistake too many and came home behind his English friend Richard Faulds in the double trap.

There was bitter sweet sadness, too, when we said goodbye to the Woodies. Mark Woodforde and Todd Woodbridge said farewell as a doubles team after 10 title-winning years together. It should have been a golden farewell, yet they limped home with silver after being beaten in a tie breaker by the Canadians.

And there were the high moments of good sportsmanship. The applause and sudden fame for "Eric the Eel", the African swimmer who could barely make it to the end of the pool. The standing applause for the Cambodian runner who finished number 80, second last in the men's marathon.

But of all the images and the memories, the one that will endure forever is what occurred at 8.10pm on Monday September 25.

Cathy Freeman ran.

Cathy Freeman won the women's 400m.

For this, above all, made the millenium Olympic Games a memory to cherish forever. It made the Sydney 2000 Olympic Games, Cathy's Games.

Freeman floated to golden glory and into Australia's honor roll, carried on the wings of sound by the choir of over 100,000 voices, playing an Australian ode to joy as she ran.

She was wearing a green and silver Phantom like running suit as she flew. But this was no ghost who walks, rather the spirit of Australia, running with the bounding grace of a kangaroo in full flight In just 49.11 seconds it was all over. Then she just sat down on the red track, a victim of shock, unable to smile or even cry as the significance of the previous minute sank in. She simply took her shoes off, and sat there.

Gradually the realisation of what she had achieved began to sink in. Her competitors reached down and patted her on the shoulders. As the cacophony went on and on, and on, she rose. She was given an Australian flag and an Aboriginal flag. She mingled them, then began to dance down the track.

Jogging now, she came down the straight and skipped a barrier to kiss her mother, touch her brother crying into a cloth.

The Australian and Aboriginal flags were now so tightly tangled it would be hard to separate them.

Reconciliation was reality at last. The Games had won.

OPENING CEREMONY

WORDS | MIRANDA DEVINE

OPENING CEREMONY

A capacity crowd of 110,000 people, a record Australian television audience of over 10 million and 2.5 billion viewers around the world witnessed magic at Sydney Olympic Park. They were taken on a journey reflecting Australia's rich cultural and spiritual history.

Above: Cathy Freeman surprised a packed crowd to light the Olympic Cauldron.

Opposite: Australia's Aboriginal culture and heritage played a significant role in the Opening Ceremony. The Awakening started the Dreamtime sequence.

Opening spread: A sea of flowers marked the celebration of nature.

When Cathy Freeman walked on water to light Sydney's Olympic Cauldron it seemed the most fitting finale to an Opening Ceremony that was suffused with a haunting Aboriginal spirituality.

The crowd roared its approval of a show that combined the thundering hooves of 120 stockhorses, burning eucalyptus, tapdancers in work-boots, fire-breathing stiltwalkers and giant Ned Kellys, along with a traditional smoke-filled Aboriginal cleansing ceremony of the stadium ground.

Apart from the popular Aboriginal sprinter, there were three stars of the night. One was Hero Girl, Nikki Webster, a tiny 13-year-old in a pink sundress who flew 30m above the stadium floor. Another was The Songman, Arnhem Land Aborigine Djakapurra Munyarryun, who drew 1000 Aboriginal dancers into the stadium to the sound of a heartbeat and didgeridoo.

And there was the audience. The 110,000 people packed into the Olympic Stadium were involved in the show like no other Olympic crowd before them. They waved yellow torches and glowing wristbands. People in the southern stand also helped stage one of the loveliest, and most risky, moments of the evening, by dragging an enormous white flag over their heads, down into the stadium.

As the flag moved slowly down the stand, you could see the rippling of thousands of helping hands underneath, as images of athletes and a white dove of peace were projected on to it. But the crowd's biggest contribution was their strong lungs which were exercised with a collective "G'day" to country singer John Williamson's Waltzing Matilda. When Williamson stopped singing and let the crowd carry the chorus, for a few spine-tingling moments, 110,000 voices sang, word-perfect, the alternative national anthem.

And for a show of national pride, there was nothing louder than the roar that filled the stadium when the Australian Olympic team entered the ground, at the end of the parade of 11,000 athletes from 199 nations. Fortunately, what was never heard was the sound of cringing from the audience. Director Ric Birch's fourth Olympic show was distinctively, assertively Australian, with corrugated iron and woodchopping, Akubras and Drizabones.

OPENING CEREMONY

There were no kangaroos on bikes but there were still plenty of in-jokes: Victa lawnmowers and, of course, the outdoor dunnies.

The show began with a Man From Snowy River welcome by 120 stockhorses galloped in by riders, aged from 15 to 77, wearing Drizabones, moleskins and Akubras, carrying first Olympic flags, then Australian flags.

Then, in the first of seven segments telling the story of Australia, the Hero Girl, with her strawberry blonde ringlets, walked into the middle of the stadium, and fell asleep on a giant beachtowel.

Her dreams formed the opening sequence, Deep Sea Dreaming, in which giant diaphanous sea creatures, from prawns and stingrays to anemones, a barracouta, and even a wriggling green worm on a hook, floated around the stadium.

Hero Girl flew high above the ground on near-invisible wires and started swimming in the air.

Suddenly, the atmosphere turned spooky as Awakening began, with the grey ghostly shapes of body-painted Arnhem Land dancers clustered in the middle of the stadium's vast brown dirt floor, and the haunting sound of the didgeridoo.

There was a colorful series of five floats with hundreds of singers and dancers representing the waves of migration which helped build the nation.

Dancers wearing steel-soled workboots, and checked shirts, tap-dancing their way into the centre of the stadium, Tap-Dogs style.

Fireworks formed the image of the Harbour Bridge, with the familiar looping word Eternity, just as it was on New Year's Eve. Then there was the stirring sound of the Marching Bands, the final act before the parade of nations.

The suspense was palpable when Betty Cuthbert entered the stadium, the Olympic torch strapped to her wheelchair, pushed by Raelene Boyle.

Who would light the cauldron? When Cathy Freeman took the flame, it seemed so obvious.

For the 2.5 billion audience worldwide, the Opening Ceremony will have showcased an admirable Australian identity forged from the ancient sprituality of Aborigines and the resourceful optimism of the migrants who joined them in their strange brown land.

For freshly patriotic Australians, it was like looking at yourself in the mirror and really liking what you see.

Above: 'G'day world' was a recurring theme throughout the entertainment, and also among the crowd as Australia waited to welcome 198 other nations to Sydney. The crowd waving flashlights and fluorescent wristbands, was part of the ceremony throughout the night.

Left: Dancers worked together to form intricate shapes, including some of Australia's wildflowers.

Opposite: Stilt walkers made a huge impact on the capacity crowd.

Right: Australian flagbearer and five-time Olympian Andrew Gaze could not contain his joy.

Top: A moment of history. North and South Korea marched in the Opening Ceremony as one team.

Above: Several athletes wore national costume, including Mongolian judo athlete B. Bat-Erdene.

Opposite, top: The Ned Kellys looked like a great Australian work of art.

Opposite, far left: 13-year-old Nikki Webster stole the show with her dream walk through Australian culture.

Opposite, right, centre: Captain Cook came, saw and discovered.

Opposite, right, bottom: Australian stockmen paraded with the IOC flag.

Above: Cathy Freeman kept her part in the Opening Ceremony secret for four months. Many Australian fans already believe she can walk on water.

Left: At the top of the stadium and on top of the world — Australian fans were out in force celebrating the start of the Games.

Opposite, top left: The world's biggest marching band filled the stadium with sound.

Opposite, top right: John Farnham and Olivia Newton-John sang up a storm.

Opposite, far left, centre and bottom: The wheels of Australian industry and a tribute to sheep and the shearer.

Bottom right: Australia's gifts to the world included the motor mower.

SWIMMING

SWIMMING

Thunderous home town support fired Australia to its best Olympic result in the pool since Munich, with the new generation swimmers leading the charge. The rest of the world also signalled they too are a force, amply demonstrated by the powerful Dutch team.

Above: Australia's male and female swimmers of the Olympic Games were, without doubt, Ian Thorpe and Susie O'Neill.

Opening spread: An awesome sight, in awesome form – Dutch superstar Pieter van den Hoogenband.

It promised a battle royale between the United States of America and Australia for the title of world's leading swimming nation, a battle that was over almost before it had started, when the host nation's brave early salvo was answered with a crashing artillery barrage.

By way of compensation, however, the Sydney 2000 Olympic Games swimming competition did turn on a spectacular Dutch treat and so many world records — 14 bettered, one equalled in 32 events, the most since 1976 — that by week's end there were light-hearted calls for a tape measure to check that the pool had not been built a metre short. And no, it hadn't.

Close as the venue itself came to becoming the star of the show, with US team veterans Lenny Krayzelburg and Amy van Dyken describing it as the fastest pool in the world, it was the Dutch "royal couple" of Pieter van den Hoogenband and Inge de Bruijn who proved to be the real scene-stealers. It was not just that she took three gold and he two; it was the manner in which they did so — displaying astounding speed in the water and admirable poise out of it.

"Inky", as de Bruijn came to be known, was especially tested. It was not so much by her rivals whom she beat with consummate ease, but by the snide suggestions that her performances were enhanced by more than Dutch courage and determination.

Such allegations have become almost the staple of Olympic swimming competitions. In Seoul, accusing fingers were pointed at the East Germans, no-one suspecting the 1988 Games would be their last hurrah. In Barcelona, it was the Chinese who drew suspicions; in Atlanta, triple Irish gold medallist Michelle Smith.

Sadly, in all three cases, those suspicions proved to be well-founded, but de Bruijn does not appear to fit the profile of a drug cheat.

After all, why, if she was so fanatical to win gold, had she withdrawn from the Atlanta Olympic Games through lack of interest? It makes no sense.

What did make sense was the crowd's open-hearted and generous acceptance of her astonishing achievements. The Australian spectators decided her three world records in the 100m butterfly and the two freestyle sprints were swims to be celebrated, not scorned.

Grant Hackett and Kieren Perkins gave Australia the race that stopped a nation in the 1500m freestyle. All the pressure that Hackett had felt during the lead-in evaporated the instant he touched the wall, more than a body length ahead of the two-time Olympic gold medallist. Hackett led from the start and said later he felt comfortable about his race after the first 100m. Rivalry between the two has been strong since the 20-year-old emerged after the Atlanta Olympic Games, but the sportsmanship between them is now also legendary.

Above: The Americans boldly predicted the Australian 4x100m freestyle relay team would be "smashed like guitars", but Chris Fydler, Ashley Callus, Michael Klim and Ian Thorpe decided to play a different tune. After a brilliant lead-off leg from Klim in which he broke the world record, Australia had the best possible start. Despite strong challenges from the US, Fydler and Callus kept coming back to ensure Australia maintained a slender buffer. Then, the final leg, Thorpe against renowned American sprinter Gary Hall Jr. The crowd raised the roof as Thorpe refused to be cowed by the fast-finishing American. He touched out the Atlanta 100m sprint silver medallist, handing the US its first defeat in the 4x100m freeestyle relay in Olympic history.

Above: The crucial final changeover as Ashley Callus touches the wall. Thorpe times it to perfection to anchor the 4x100m freestyle relay.

Below left: A relieved Ian Thorpe mouthed "thank you" in the pool after his 400m freestyle win, but out of the pool, it was a different matter.

Below right: Swim legends embrace. Dawn Fraser can't resist grabbing teen sensation and triple gold medallist Ian Thorpe poolside for a hug.

Even more of that generosity of spirit was extended to van den Hoogenband after the Dutchman pulled off the first of the meet's three stunning upsets, all of them at the expense of the Australians.

For one brief moment, it seemed that 17,500 spectators simultaneously had been struck dumb after van den Hoogenband touched out hometown hero Ian Thorpe to win the 200m freestyle gold.

But then shock and disappointment gave way to an appreciation of what the 22-year-old medical student from the tiny village of Geldrop had achieved. And in the next moment, Pieter the Great was being accorded a standing ovation.

By the time the 100m freestyle rolled around, the Dutchman well and truly had lost the element of surprise. All the more credit to him, then, for the manner in which he outswam and out-touched

Russian Alexander Popov in the final, denying Australia's adopted son the honor of becoming the first man ever to win the same event at three consecutive Games.

Popov had one last chance to achieve the feat, in the 50m freestyle, but after surfacing from his dive marginally ahead of the field, the world record holder was trampled in the stampede.

He finished sixth in a race that resulted in an historic dead-heat between Americans Gary Hall Jr and Anthony Ervin for the gold with "Hoogie" taking the bronze.

Hall Jr revelled in the "villain" role assigned to him by the Australian spectators, who booed him good-naturedly every time he appeared, their boos quickly degenerating into laughter as the American showman won them over with his playful antics. But Hall's pre-meet boast that the Americans would smash the Australians

"like guitars" had looked pretty lame on Day One of competition.

Thorpe, anything but fresh from his world record-breaking gold medal triumph in the 400m freestyle, swam over the top of Hall to pull off a mesmerising Australian victory in the 4x100m freestyle relay, the first time in Olympic history the USA had been defeated in the event.

Thorpe's anchor leg was exhilarating but it was the 100m freestyle world record set by Michael Klim in the opening leg, backed up by the courageous input of Chris Fydler and Ashley Callus, that allowed The Thorpedo to sink the Americans.

The Australians were crowing after plucking the tail-feathers of the American eagle, but it was a victory that was to prove very costly in the long run. Everyone cheers when David sneaks one through Goliath's defences, but the far more predictable scenario is that

Goliath unloads a backhander that sends David reeling. And so it proved once the Americans had been stung into action. The US response was savage.

There were golden doubles from glamor backstroker Krayzelburg and distance queen Brooke Bennett; a world record-breaking swim by Tom Dolan to retain his 400m individual medley title; the emergence of 16-year-old 100m breaststroker Megan Quann to trump Australia's 15-year-old Leisel Jones; and three relay golds that propelled Jenny Thompson to her 10th Olympic medal — making her the most prolific female swimming medal winner in Games history.

But by far the most devastating "payback" came in the women's 200m butterfly final. This was to be the crowning moment of Susie O'Neill's career.

For the six years leading into these Games, no-one but countrywoman Petria Thomas had ever threatened her in this event and even Thomas knew she would need a miracle to finish with anything better than silver.

The Americans had Misty Hyman, of course, but everyone knew that her race would follow the same predictable pattern of the last three years — leading at the 150m mark, then dying spectacularly over

Top left: Relay mania on the last day of swimming with the 4x100m medley relays for men and women. Team USA took out the men's event in world record time.

Top right: Michael Klim, Geoff Huegill, Regan Harrison and Matt Welsh almost allowed the boxing kangaroo to accept their silver medals.

Above left: The American women also won in world record time. For Jenny Thompson (second from left), it was an incredible eighth gold medal, all in relays.

Above: Leisel Jones, Dyana Calub, Petria Thomas and Susie O'Neill also broke the world record to claim silver.

Opposite page: Australia's swim team gave thanks after the close of competition.

Right: Dutch treat. Inge De Bruijn completed an unprecendented golden treble with the 50m freestyle on the final day of swimming. She also claimed gold in the 100m freestyle and 100m butterfly, all in world record time.

Opposite page: The other superstar of swimming also wore the colors of the Netherlands. Pieter van den Hoogenband was unbeatable in the blue riband event, the 100m freestyle, much to the disappointment of Australia's Michael Klim and Russian Alexander Popov, who was going for a third successive Olympic gold in the event.

Above: The Australian connection was strong with Italian gold medallist Massimiliano Rosolino, celebrating his 200m Individual Medley victory. Rosolino's mother is Australian and his grandmother still lives in Melbourne. He spent several years of his childhood here.

Opposite: A perfect start for the field in the men's 100m freestyle.

the final lap. This one time, however, Hyman stayed very much alive and O'Neill realised too late that she could not rely on the American collapsing under the pressure.

She lifted, as a true champion always will when confronted by a challenge, but the wall was too close. Hyman claimed the gold and O'Neill was left ruefully kicking herself for not having allowed herself to celebrate her 200m freestyle triumph earlier in the meet.

"If I had known that was to be my only gold medal, I would have celebrated a lot more," O'Neill said.

Nonetheless, the Australian finished the meet with one gold and three silvers to lift her career tally to eight, equalling Dawn Fraser's record for the most Olympic medals won by an Australian.

Yet the tally that mattered most was the final medal count of the competing nations. Having pushed the Americans right down

to the wire at Pan Pacs one year earlier in this same pool, the Australians were entitled to entertain hopes of lowering the Star SpangledBbanner at these Games.

But the Olympic Games are a meet like no other and no prize in sport is more desperately pursued than an Olympic gold medal. Thorpe, despite winning three golds and two silvers, discovered that when he was ambushed by the Flying Dutchman; so too O'Neill when Misty rained on her parade; and so, again, did Klim and Geoff Huegill when the cool Swede, Lars Froelander, suddenly got hot in the 100m butterfly final. Had those three golds not slipped through their fingers, the Australians might have made more of a fight of their challenge to the USA. Ultimately, however, the Olympic Games confirmed America's No.1 standing, its 14 golds and 33 medals easily eclipsing Australia's five golds, nine silvers and four bronzes.

But at least the Australians saved their best until last. When the final day of competition dawned, Australia was a nation on tenterhooks. Could Kieren Perkins win his third successive 1500m freestyle gold? Could he achieve, in swimming's longest and most gruelling event, what Popov had been unable to do in the two sprints?

Or would Grant Hackett, his earlier form ragged and unconvincing, keep intact his unbeaten four-year record in the event? Or the unthinkable — would one of the Americans, Erik Vendt or Chris Thompson, or Russian Alexei Filperts or South African Ryk Neethling, deny their hosts the one gold medal they desired most of all?

The gun sounded. The race started. The nation stopped.

Hackett led out, pursued by Perkins. It was on — the ultimate showdown in what developed into the fastest 1500m race of all time, world champion versus world record holder and Olympic champion. The crowd refused to play favorites, chanting "Aussie, Aussie". At the 700m mark, Perkins decided he must make his move. It was now or never, he decided, planting the accelerator.

It turned out to be "never". Hackett answered the challenge. As he turned for the final lap, Perkins eight strokes behind, the crowd stood as one. They were not just saluting the new champion, but the old one as well. Perkins handed to Hackett the responsibility of keeping intact Australia's unbeaten record in the event, a record that stretches back to 1991.

The final individual swimming race of the Sydney Olympic Games ended just as it had in Barcelona and Atlanta, with Australians standing on the top two steps of the victory dais. It was, said Perkins, the perfect result.

And the perfect way to bring down the curtain on the greatest swim meet ever held on these shores.

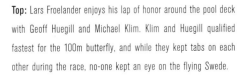

Top: Lars Froelander enjoys his lap of honor around the pool deck with Geoff Huegill and Michael Klim. Klim and Huegill qualified fastest for the 100m butterfly, and while they kept tabs on each other during the race, no-one kept an eye on the flying Swede.

Above: Immediately after the race, Huegill and Klim looked back at the scoreboard, almost in disbelief. Klim claimed silver while Huegill took his first Olympic medal, a bronze.

Above right: To the winner, the bragging rights.

Opposite: Americans Anthony Ervin and Gary Hall Jr celebrate that rarest of feats, a dead-heat to claim dual gold in the 50m freestyle. It was the first gold medal for Hall, who claimed silver behind Alexander Popov in Atlanta.

Above: American Misty Hyman proudly shows off her gold medal in the 200m butterfly, while placegetters Susie O'Neill and Petria Thomas head for the dressing rooms.

Opposite, top left: Italy's Domenico Fioravanti celebrates his win in the 200m breaststroke.

Opposite, top right: Megan Quann had plenty to holler about after edging out Leisel Jones in the 100m breaststroke final.

Opposite, middle right: You don't have to win gold to experience sheer elation. Just ask 200m butterfly bronze medallist, Australia's Justin Norris.

Opposite, below left: Anxiety shows on the faces of Susie O'Neill, Giaan Rooney and Kirsten Thomson as Petria Thomas swims the final leg of the 4x200m freestyle relay, won by the USA.

Opposite, below right: Petria Thomas enjoys a kiss from Scott Volkers after helping Australia to silver in the freestyle relay.

Above: Madame and Mademoiselle Butterfly – Susie O'Neill just has the edge on Petria Thomas in the semi-finals of the 200m butterfly.

Right: An unexpected gold. Susie O'Neill tried to claim that the 200m freestyle was not her distance, but it seems the rest of the world wasn't listening.

Opposite, top: Eric Moussambani won his heat of the 100m freestyle in 1:52.72. Moussambani, from Equatorial Guinea, had never swum in a 50m pool before and swam alone in his heat after two other competitors were disqualified for false starts. Struggling to finish, the crowd roared support for the man who learned to swim just nine months ago and received a wild card entry into the Olympic Games.

Opposite, bottom left: Moussambi immediately became a celebrity, scoring a new fastskin swimsuit to further his sporting career.

Opposite, bottom right: Melbourne-based Matt Welsh pushed American sensation Lenny Krayzelburg all the way to take silver in the 100m backstroke final.

Main picture: Todd Pearson, Michael Klim and Ian Thorpe jumped into the pool to celebrate the world record-breaking win in the 4x200m freestyle relay with final swimmer Bill Kirby. The Australian team never allowed any rival a look-in after Thorpe blasted through the first leg.

Top: Klim takes over from Thorpe to ram home the advantage.

Above: Sheer elation and quiet pride. Klim and Thorpe were a study in contrasts on the pool deck.

Above: A mutual admiration society. Ian Thorpe on the dais with 200m freestyle gold medallist, Pieter van den Hoogenband of the Netherlands.

Left: The moment of truth – van den Hoogenband touches out the Thorpedo, equalling the world record he set in the semi-finals the previous night.

Opposite, main picture: Lethal Leisel – all Australia acclaimed 15-year-old Brisbane schoolgirl Leisel Jones after her gutsy second in the 100m breaststroke.

Opposite, far left: The youngest member of the Australian Olympic Team, Leisel Jones proudly shows off her silver medal.

Opposite, bottom right: All smiles from the all-powerful Dutch sprinter, Inge de Bruijn, after her gold in the 100m butterfly.

TRIATHLON

WORDS | RON REED

TRIATHLON

Making its debut as an Olympic sport, triathlon had it all — scenery, skill, determination and gut-busting effort. At the end of the day, Australia did not dominate in either the men's or women's event but the sport won the hearts and minds of sport lovers all over the world.

Above: Canadian gold medallist Simon Whitfield collapses with his national flag after scoring an upset victory.

Opposite page: Million-dollar harbor views, but the men's triathlon competitors kept their gaze firmly on the course.

Opening spread: The Australian women, Michellie Jones, Nicole Hackett and Loretta Harrop, had been favored to sweep the medals and at the final transition they looked a good chance to do it.

Of all the elements that add up to memorable sport, exciting contests decided only in the final few minutes or metres are hard to beat. In that case, the feisty new-age sport of triathlon can be fully satisfied with its Olympic debut and should be able to look forward to a permanent place on the program.

The women and men both turned on thrillers that drew crowds estimated at 300,000, and that's a powerful point for any first timer to make.

So while the International Triathlon Union and its fast-talking president, Canada's Les McDonald, will have to wait until the International Olympic Committee reviews its status, it will be a major shock if we do not see these superb all-rounders swimming their 1500m, cycling for 40km and running for 10km in Athens in 2004.

If anything was missing — and it wasn't ideal weather or the best scenery Sydney's beautiful harbor precinct has to offer — it was a gold medal for Australia, a surprise given that only a year earlier the Australian women had filled the first five places at the world championships and the men had been consistent podium performers. But in different ways, the hosts weren't entirely bereft of glory.

The men's winner, Simon Whitfield, is a Canadian and deeply proud of it, but he holds dual citizenship because his father is Australian and it was all he could do to hold back tears when asked at his victory press conference to explain his feelings about the Australian connection. And at the end of a race lasting over two hours there were a mere two seconds separating Australia's Michellie Jones from the women's gold medal, which she found disappointing for all of another two seconds. Then she grinned and exclaimed: "Winning an Olympic silver medal for Australia — that ain't bad".

As much as anything, that seemed to sum up the feel-good, friendly mood of two days that helped erase the memory of a troubled build-up, which saw the world championship farcically contested over a wrongly-measured course in Perth, injuries and illness making life hard for some of Australia's top performers and then a long and expensive dispute over the selection of the women's team.

In the end, Switzerland emerged as the most successful nation, with Brigitte McMahon and

Magali Messmer taking gold and bronze in the women's event, Whitfield earning Canada a gold and Germany's Stephan Vuckovic and the Czech Republic's Jan Rehula collecting the minor men's medals.

The women's race was almost a duplicate of the World Cup event over the same course in April, except that Jones won that one ahead of McMahon. And when the Californian-based dual world champion left the final transition marginally in the lead, her renowned running skills looked like being the decisive factor again, especially as she was carrying the No.1 world ranking against McMahon's 21.

What transpired, however, was a stupendous duel that began 15 minutes or so from the finish, with McMahon setting a cracking pace and Jones sitting at her shoulder, urged on by her family and friends and everyone else in the crowd, including two famous cheerleaders in swimming icons Dawn Fraser and Laurie Lawrence.

Jones momentarily inched past but her legs were sending her heart a message in three letters: SOS. She knew she wasn't going to make it, while McMahon simply thought about what a wonderful story this was going to make for her infant son and duly prevailed.

Australia's other two competitors, Loretta Harrop and Nicole Hackett, finished fifth and ninth after failing to get their usual jump on the field in the swim leg, unable to explain later what went wrong. There was nothing to confirm it and they certainly didn't offer it as an excuse, but it was difficult to escape the suspicion that they weren't helped by being caught up in the middle of a four month selection dispute which ended only a few days before the Games opened.

Whitfield's triumph was no less dramatic than McMahon's, it was just shaped differently. Instead of holding a rival at bay, he swooped from behind to chase down a tiring Vuckovic within the last 100 metres or so of a race that had many leaders during the ride and the run. If you thought he was happy, you were right, but the powerful, chrome-domed German might have been even more pleased with his silver, grabbing a national flag from out of the crowd and prancing with it down the final

few metres, high-fiving the spectators in a manner made famous by Australia's Peter Robertson in the World Cup.

Vuckovic ran second to the colorful Robbo that day so it is not difficult to see where he was coming from with his antics. Robertson, though, had an ordinary day, finishing 34th while Australia's Miles Stewart was pleased with his sixth and Craig Walton settled for 27th after leading throughout the first half of the race.

But Whitfield was the story, even for the Australian media. His father Geoff, a scientist, is Australian and so is his 96-year- old grandmother who still lives just the other side of the bridge, and he holds dual citizenship. Between 1992 and 1996, he went to his father's old school in Sydney, Knox Grammar, where he reckons the lessons he learned best were about toughness and competitiveness.

Triathlon was something he picked up on too, especially when he was befriended by Greg Bennett, a star Australian athlete who was to be one of the unlucky victims of the rule that only three can go to the Games from any one country. Australian officials had tried to persuade Whitfield to stay, an ironic situation when so many Australians have moved elsewhere in bids to gain Olympic selection.

Whitfield wore his emotions on his sleeve when talking about what has become his second home, saying: "I am deeply, deeply proud to be a Canadian, but there is a little bit of my heart that belongs to Australia."

Only a bit, though. Whitfield's excitement at the medal presentation was even more obvious than it was at the finish line. "People kept asking me what my goal was and all I ever said was that I wanted to hear my anthem," he said. "When I did, it knocked me out." That's when he knew that no matter how much of his heart belongs to Australia, his blood still flowed red and white.

Above: Michellie Jones had huge home town pressure going into the first medal event of the Games, and gave her all to come home with silver.

Left: Anyone competing at the Olympic Games can be a winner – just ask the Netherlands' Rob Barel.

Opposite: The Canadian press didn't rate Simon Whitfield any chance of upsetting a class field. Whitfield outlasted a bevy of European runners to take the gold.

Top: To the Swiss, the spoils. Brigitte McMahon and Magali Messmer celebrate with their flag.

Right: There is nothing like a gold. An elated Brigitte McMahon breaks the tape, while a spent Michellie Jones staggers to the finish line to claim Australia's first medal.

Top left: Miles Stewart, who finished sixth, needed to call on all his gritty reserves to chase down the leading pack on the bike.

Top: Loretta Harrop did not dominate as expected in the swim leg and left the first transition with Michellie Jones hot on her heels.

Above: The final tussle among the men. Simon Whitfield just gets past Stephan Vukovic (right) and the Czech Republic's Jan Rehula (back).

Left: The spectacular start at Farm Cove, just off the Sydney Opera House steps.

ARCHERY

The South Korean influence in the Olympic archery tournament was fully expected. Its impact on the Australian team, however, was not. Simon Fairweather and his South Korean coach combined in Sydney to produce their own chapter in the chronicles of Olympic glory.

Above: The emotion hits Simon Fairweather at his medal ceremony.

Opposite: The moment of triumph. Fairweather becomes Australia's first medallist in archery, and caps off a great career with a gold.

Australia's first ever Olympic medal in archery came from an unlikely combination, an athlete with a tortured soul and a South Korean mastermind. Simon Fairwearther was unstoppable in winning an historic gold in the men's individual event, giving most of the credit to his coach of three years, Ki Sik Lee.

Mr Lee, as he is known by his small band of elite Australian archers, had guided the South Korean team to a swag of medals at four previous Olympic Games. This time, his guidance proved the difference for Australia.

Lee's programs continue to be used in his homeland and were also largely responsible for South Korea's domination in this Olympic Games. South Korea set two world and eight Olympic records on its way to winning the men's and women's team events, as well as sweeping the medals in the women's individual competition. But Lee ensured his countrymen fell short of a clean sweep by lifting local hero and four-time Olympian Fairweather to glory.

A decade ago, Fairweather was at the top of his sport, winning the 1991 world championship. He was feted, but then he flopped at his first three Olympic Games and seriously considered retirement after Atlanta. He knew, though, he would be wasting one of the most prolific talents in the archery world and thankfully, the lure of a home Games was too strong.

Fairweather rode a wave of emotion and frenzied support from his home crowd to win six knockout matches, culminating in a pulsating 113-106 victory over American Vic Wunderle in the gold medal shoot-off. The 30-year-old had been pushed far harder in the semi-final by bronze medallist Wietse Van Alten, from the Netherlands, but held his cool to nail two bullseyes to finish for a 112-110 victory. In the quarter-finals he had overpowered Russian world no.5 Baljinima Tsyrempilov 113-104. Fairweather's total score for the three final matches equalled the Olympic record of 338 set by South Korean Oh Kyo Moon in Atlanta.

So deadly was Fairweather's eye, that of the 90 arrows he let fly, 41 were bullseyes and 37 landed just wide of perfection in the nine-point ring. It was an incredible display of precision and concentration in the blustery winds of Homebush Bay for a man standing 70 metres

from the target, aiming at a bullseye that looked about the size of a thumbnail.

"Everyone kept telling me it was my day but I tried to not to think to hard about it," a stunned Fairweather said after his victory. "I just kept on trying to think about my process and my technique. When I won the world championships in 1991 that was the sort of mindset I was in, just stick to the shooting part of it and not worry about the results. And I guess in the years in between I've had trouble doing that, isolating the performance from the results. It's a great lesson for anyone — just stick to your process and not worry about other people's expectations."

The gold medal was the ultimate in satisfaction for Fairweather after he struggled to cope with the cut throat pressure of matchplay competition,

introduced at the 1992 Olympic Games to make the sport more spectator-friendly. Before that, archers stood in a long line and shot their arrows together with the winner being the one who totalled the most points.

From the little town of Strathalbyn, just outside Adelaide, Fairweather just could not get his mind around the radical change and struggled against the world's best ever since, until Sydney. It was Lee who pulled apart Fairweather's technique and mental approach and put it back together. He fashioned Fairweather into a competitor capable of again matching it with the best. His younger sister Kate, also on the Olympic archery team, said there was no more deserving victor than her brother.

South Korea's men's team were as dominant as Fairweather. The archery powerhouse won its first gold medal in the

teams since 1988, with Oh Kyo Moon, Jang Yong Ho and Kim Chung Tae thumping world champion Italy 255-247 in the final. The US took the bronze after an extra-arrow win over Russia. In the women's team event, South Korea's Yun Mi Jin, Kim Nam Soon and Kim Soo Nyung notched a world record in qualifying, scoring 1994 points from a possible 2160, and another world mark for the the 54-arrow finals total of 502, on their way to winning gold ahead of Ukraine and Germany. In individual competition, Yun, the youngest competitor in the event at just 17, led a clean sweep by holding her nerve in the gold medal shoot-off to beat countrywoman Kim Nam Soon 107-106. Yun went into the last of her 12 arrows knowing she needed at least nine to win the match and did it with aplomb. The bronze went to veteran Kim Soo Nyung.

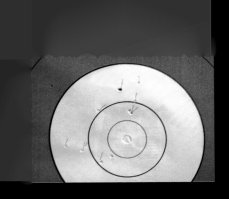

Right: Concentration and nerve kept Simon Fairweather on target.

Top: What everyone is aiming for – a bullseye.

Above, middle: Michelle Tremelling put in a creditable performance in the women's team and individual events.

Above: Australian archers enjoyed rabid support at Sydney Archery Park.

Opposite, top: The sheer spectacle of archery, the arrow leaving the bow, captured in slow motion.

Opposite, far left: Korea's Mi Jin Yun takes the women's individual event.

Opposite, left: Celebrations for Korea's first medal since 1988 in the men's team event.

WORDS | ANDREW CAPEL

SHOOTING

Australia's shooting team had to keep its nerve in a highly-pressured environment. The team came through with a haul of five goals, to equal its best-ever Olympic result, led by an emotion-charged Michael Diamond, who dedicated his second successive gold to his late father, Con.

Above: Brothers in arms. Russell Mark gives Michael Diamond some encouragement going into the final of the men's single trap.

Opposite page: A second successive Olympic gold to Michael Diamond in the trap. The elation later gave way to tears as Diamond dedicated his victory to his father and mentor, Con, who died in May this year.

From the ecstasy of Michael Diamond's gold medal, to the despair of heartbreaking shoot-off losses to Russell Mark and Tash Lonsdale. The Australian shooting team had more than its share of excitement and drama at the Olympic Games. Its result of three medals, a gold, silver and bronze placed Australia fifth on the shooting medals count and equalled its best-ever medal haul, in Atlanta four years ago.

Until Atlanta, Australia had won just three medals in shooting in Olympic history.

By retaining his men's trap crown in front of a passionate home crowd, Diamond established himself as the greatest clay target shooter of all time.

He became the first Australian to win two gold medals in shooting by hitting a perfect round of 75 shots in the final. Diamond won by an astonishing five — the equivalent of winning a 400m swim by the length of the pool.

Only one other shooter, Italy's Luciano Giovanetti in 1980 and '84, had previously won two gold medals in clay target shooting, against vastly-inferior opposition.

"With the two Olympic golds, world cups and world championships Michael has won, I don't think anyone could dispute that he is the greatest clay target shooter the world has seen," said Australian clay target coach, Greg Chan.

Diamond's remarkable victory was one of the stories of the Games. He had made it his mission to win a second gold after losing his dad, coach and mentor Con Diamond to illness in May.

"This one was for Dad," said Diamond.

"He was my power force and I thought, 'bugger it, he didn't teach me for 20 years to just walk out there and fail'."

While buoyed by Diamond's win and satisfied with its medal return, the feeling among the Australian team was that it was a Games of lost opportunities.

Mark, like Diamond, was chasing a second consecutive Olympic gold medal but he threw away victory in the men's double trap. It was an uncharacteristic loss of control in the closing stages of the final. After setting a new Olympic record of 143 out of 150 in the qualifying rounds, the usually cool and collected Mark missed four of his last 11 targets in

Above: Shooter Annemarie Forder has an affinity for metal — particularly for the bronze variety.
Right: Forder in action in the women's 10m air pistol.

Opposite page: A picture of perfect concentration. Michael Diamond shot a clean round of 75 hits to claim gold in the trap.

the final to virtually hand the gold to Great Britain's Richard Faulds, losing in a sudden-death shoot-off. He surrendered what would usually have been an unassailable three-target advantage with 10 shots remaining by inexplicably missing a pair of targets on his third-last series — the first time he had missed a pair since March.

"This is nightmare stuff," Mark said. "There are no excuses. I had my chances to win and I blew it."

Mark claimed Australia's first silver medal in Olympic shooting.

The shoot-off came back to haunt Australia for a second time when 22-year-old women's skeet shooter Tash Lonsdale, who describes herself as "the little Aussie battler", missed a bronze medal in similar heart-rending circumstances.

She powered her way into the final with a personal-best qualifying score of 70 out of 75 before missing one target in the shoot-off and losing the bronze to Hungary's Diana Igaly.

The big disappointment for Australia was the failure of women's trap and double trap shooter Deserie Wakefield-Baynes, who was expected to win medals in both events.

She failed to make the final of either, crumbling under the weight of expectation and home crowd pressure and breaking down in tears even before she shot in her second event.

One shooter who did not crack was Gold Coast pistol exponent 22-year-old Annemarie Forder, who shot her way into the history books by becoming Australia's first air pistol medallist in 104 years of Olympic competition.

She won bronze in the women's 10m air pistol event after a stunning last shot of 10.5 in the final which propelled her above Russian world recordholder Svetlana Smirnova and into the medals.

China dominated the medal tally with eight, including three golds, while the biggest failure was the traditionally-strong German team which did not win a medal.

Its two superstars, Ralf Schumann and Sonja Pfeilschifter, were two of the competition's biggest failures.

Schumann, aiming to become the first man to win three shooting gold medals, managed only fifth place in the men's rapid fire pistol.

Pfeilschifter was unable to break her Olympic medal drought, shooting poorly in the finals of the women's 50m rifle three position and 10m air rifle events to finish fourth and fifth respectively.

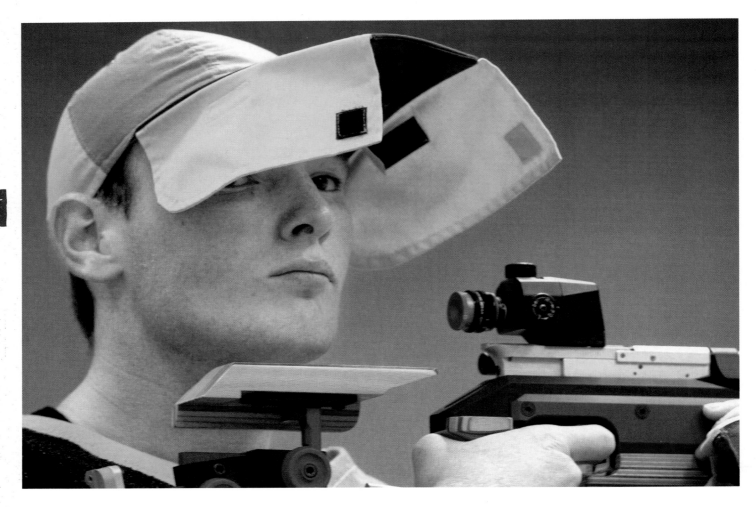

Above: Timothy Lowndes tried to continue Australia's fine record in shooting in the 50m Prone Rifle, finishing 19th.
Left: A favorite for gold, Australia's Deserie Wakefield-Baynes was consoled by coach Luca Scribani Rossi after failing to make the final of the women's trap.

Opposite: A rare double miss cost Russell Mark dearly, forcing him into a shoot-off for gold in the double trap. He finished with silver behind Great Britain's Richard Faulds.
Opposite, bottom left: Mark's two-year-old daughter Holly got a taste of her dad's silver medal.
Opposite, bottom right: Briton Richard Faulds celebrates after winning the double trap shoot-off.

Above: Once of the world's richest men, Prince Jefri, a brother to the Sultan of Brunei, contested the men's skeet.

Left: France's Franck Dumoulin shoots for gold in the 10m air pistol.

Opposite page, main picture: Tash Lonsdale describes herself as "the little Aussie battler". She lost a heart-rending shoot-off for bronze in the women's skeet final.

Opposite, top right: American Nancy Johnson scored the first gold of the Sydney 2000 shooting competition, winning the 10m air rifle.

Opposite, bottom right: Sweden's Pia Hansen celebrates victory in the women's double trap.

BADMINTON

They are star-crossed lovers, with the badminton world at their feet. But celebrity and glamor could not ensure Camilla Martin and Peter Gade matching Olympic gold medals. They, like all other players, had to bow to the might of the Chinese.

Above: It was a common sight — a Chinese celebration. Xingpeng Ji swept away all comers to claim the men's singles gold.

Opposite, below left: China's Jun Zhang belts an overhead smash.

Opposite, far right: The relentless Chinese kept it going in the women's doubles, winning all three medals. Jun Gu and Fei Ge took the gold.

The romantics were hoping for a warm and fuzzy fairytale, but the ending was very much cold and clinical.

China, so focused and professional, ensured Danish lovers Camilla Martin and Peter Gade would not quinella the singles gold medals.

Badminton's answer to the Andre Agassi-Steffi Graf union has spent two years dodging the Danish tabloid press, but the pair could not avoid the relentless Chinese at this Olympic Games.

Second-seeded Martin settled for silver after stumbling against China's Zhichao Gong 13-10 11-3 and her boyfriend Gade struck double Chinese trouble.

Gade, world No.1 and seeded third in the men's singles at the Games, lost to China's eventual winner Xingpeng Ji in the semis, and when bronze loomed as a consolation, Ji's teammate Xuanze Xia joined in as party pooper.

Gade fell in 37 minutes, despite leading 13-9 in the crucial opening game, to eventually lose 13-15.

It was a prime example of the Chinese domination at a pavilion packed to the rafters with Asian fans.

China won four of the five gold medals on offer, sinking only from the men's doubles without a trace. The battling Australians can only dream of such domination.

The final medal tally of eight from 15 up for grabs was a stunning improvement on Atlanta where the Chinese managed just four medals and were forced to share honors with Indonesia and Korea.

Indonesia managed just three medals in Sydney and Korea two, summing up just how much work needs to be done to catch up.

The largest Chinese cheer was reserved for Ji, who became the slayer of seeds and a shock gold medal victor in the glamor men's singles event.

Most expected the 22-year-old to vanish in the quarters, but he beat the top three seeds on the way to a shock win. Ji cleaned up Indonesian hero Henrdawan 15-4 15-13 in a 45-minute final after doing a similar job on Gade and top seed Taufik Hidayat.

As top seed, Gong's disposal of crowd favorite Martin was much less of a surprise. Martin jumped to an early lead, but had no answer when crunch time arrived in the first game. It was all downhill from there.

The Chinese domination was most pronounced in the women's doubles where all three medals went their way.

The unstoppable pair of Jun Gu and Fei Ge led the charge by cruising home 15-5 15-5 against teammates Wei Yang and Nanyan Huang, defending the gold they won at the Atlanta Olympic Games.

And there was more gold in the mixed doubles, Ling Gao and Jun Zhang belying their seventh seeding to beat top seeded Indonesian pair Tri Kusharyanto and Minarti Timur. The Chinese crumbled 1-15 in the first game, but hit back to win the final games 15-13 15-11.

Australia, full of hope in front of a parochial home crowd, bowed out of the eight-day competition within three days.

In fact, Australia could manage just one win, to women's singles specialist Rayoni Head, who rapidly crashed out in the

second round. Veterans Rhonda Cator and Peter Blackburn held match point in their first mixed doubles outing, but were cruelly denied 17-16 in the deciding game after 74 minutes.

There was just as much heartbreak in the men's singles when our main hope, Rio Suryana, squandered a seemingly match-winning lead in his first match to crash out against lowly-ranked Bulgarian

Svetoslav Stoyanov. Australian officials called an urgent meeting the morning after Suryana departed as the last Australian in the tournament.

They plan a large shake-up of the badminton program, but it will take a miracle to catch the Chinese.

Even the superpowers of the sport, including Indonesia and Denmark, are finding it difficult enough to keep up.

Above left: Danish superstar Camilla Martin could only manage silver in the singles in the face of the Chinese onslaught.

Below Left: Martin and Peter Gade, the "Andre and Steffi" of badminton, were not able to secure double golds. Gade came up against double Chinese trouble and was relegated to fourth place.

Opposite, main picture: This time, they won. Tri Kusharyanto and Minarti Timur of Indonesia show their way of celebrating a win over Germany in the mixed doubles.

Opposite, far left: Australian veteran, 34-year-old Rhonda Cator is ready to hand over to a younger generation of badminton player after a shock exit early in the women's doubles.

Opposite, bottom right: Simon Archer and Joanne Goode of Great Britain have their eyes on covering this shot.

SOFTBALL

WORDS | FIONA PURDON

SOFTBALL

Australia looked in a prime position to go better than its Atlanta bronze medal, but the efficiency of the Japanese and the uncanny ability of Team USA to come back from the dead put paid to the host nation's plans. Once again, America did what it had to do to take home the gold.

Above: The great escape. Michele Smith of the USA celebrates the gold medal.

Opposite page, top: Team USA does its victory lap of the Blacktown arena.

Opposite page, bottom: The crucial catch, spilled. Japan's Shori Koseki couldn't reel in the fly ball to left field against the USA.

Opening spread: US Pitcher Lori Hannagan directs the action against Canada in the preliminary rounds.

Predictable? The Sydney 2000 Olympic softball tournament was anything but. The inexorable march of Team USA to its second successive Olympic gold medal was stopped in its tracks — or so it seemed. In a week of upsets, only a remarkable turnaround in form saved the Americans from what, in the lead-up to Sydney, would have seemed unthinkable.

For three days running, it looked as though the world's greatest softball nation, the country that invented the game, would not be part of the gold medal playoff.

The 15-year American reign as the world's No.1 team appeared to be all but over, with Japan and Australia rising to new heights. But the Americans refused to relinquish their stranglehold, even in the face of three consecutive preliminary round defeats, at the hands of China, Japan and Australia. Even looking tentative in the minor semi-final, where defeat would have meant Olympic oblivion, the US pulled back from the brink, defeating China 3-0. That set up a showdown with Australia in the preliminary final.

For the second game in a row, the host nation's crunch big-hitting deserted it. The US went on to the gold medal game, and Australia was left to ponder another bronze. The Americans' ability to pull out incredible wins when required stood the toughest test.

Valiant Japan, unbeaten until its 2-1 loss in the gold medal game, came the closest to pushing softball's superpower — the USA team had been shaping up for its worst finish since a humbling fourth place at the 1982 world championships.

For Australia, it was a case of what might have been. No doubt the Australians were a more poised and mature team than the 1996 bronze medallists, but two 1-0 losses to Japan in the key games was not the uplifting end to the Olympic campaign the team expected.

There were gutsy performers among the Australians, especially pitchers Tanya Harding and Kelly Hardie. But, except for Peta Edebone's four home-run heroics (including three last-pitch winning hits), and a steady display by Sally McCreedy, the Australian batters did not play to their potential.

Australia finished second behind Japan after the preliminaries and it had two plum chances to progress to the gold medal game. McCreedy was the sole Australian to scrounge a hit off Japanese pitcher Marika Masubuchi in the semi-final loss, while captain Kerry Dienelt was

the only Australian to scorch a hit off American superstar Lisa Fernandez in the preliminary final.

The top four nations from Atlanta were again the standout performers in Sydney. "We performed well but there's nothing between the top four teams," McCreedy said. "We didn't get our batting together for the whole tournament, but then it hasn't been a hitting tournament. I've never been as proud to be part of a team as this one."

Despite some bizarre results, the four traditional heavyweights — Japan (seven wins), Australia (six wins and one loss), China (five wins and two losses) and United States (four wins and three losses) — not surprisingly squared off in the semi-finals. But the bottom four countries — Italy (two wins), New Zealand (two wins), Canada (one win) and Cuba (one win) — pushed

the four pacesetters. More than nine matches went to extended innings, which highlighted a closely-matched tournament.

The well-drilled Japanese, who had barely made an error all week, were undone by an outfield error in the gold medal game when Shori Koseki momentarily gloved a Laura Berg left-field fence hit but the ball slipped out as Koseki fell backwards, and the US grabbed a 2-1 lead. Japan had been poised to pull off one of the Games' biggest upsets when Reikia Utsugi, with the backing of third base coach Hiruka Saito who had decoded Lisa Fernandez's pitches, was ready for a ripe change-up pitch and smacked it for a home run in the top of the fourth inning. The United States replied with a Stacey Nuveman power centre-field hit which scored Michele Smith to equalise one-all in the bottom of the fifth inning.

Softball minnows and Olympic debutantes Cuba may have won the hearts of the crowds with their personality and feisty play, but they did upset world No. 5 Canada with a 2-1 result on the second last day of competition.

European qualifier Italy, guided by American-born pitchers Susan Buglarello and Nicole DiSalvio, also played in its first Olympic Games, upsetting New Zealand and Cuba and pushing Japan. Canada, boasting the world's second highest softball population, was beaten by a controversial Australian run when Selina Follas was called safe at home. Erin Woods thundered a seventh-inning three-run home run against Japan to force extra innings, but Canada's campaign was sunk by losses against Cuba and Olympic rookie New Zealand. New Zealand was powered by the most overworked Olympic pitcher, Gina Weber. Edebone smashed the first of her last-pitch home runs to also score Natalie Titcume and start a memorable tournament for Australia's most successful batter of the past three years.

Above: Australia takes its second straight Olympic bronze in softball.

Far left: It was Japan's best finish in softball and they celebrated by tossing their manager, Taeko Utsugi into the air.

Left: America's Sheila Douty runs out Shori Koseki during the gold medal game.

Opposite page: Australia's Fiona Hanes launches herself into the arms of home run hitter, Peta Edebone, after Edebone's last-gasp home run to sink New Zealand.

Main picture: Australia's Natalie Ward takes a great catch on second base to send American veteran Lisa Fernandez back to the dugout.

Top: The slugging form that saw Australia progress strongly through the preliminary rounds.

Above: Fiona Hanes collapses in tears, coming off the worst after a clash with America's Jennifer Brundage.

Opposite page, top: Japanese pitcher Isikawa Taeko had a day out in the preliminary round to lead in the defeat of the USA.

Opposite page, bottom: America's Jennifer Brundage gets tagged out at second base by New Zealand's Rhonda Hira.

WORDS | CAMERON BELL

FENCING

Upsets galore and a surprisingly strong performance from the host nation were no barrier to what has been described as the world's greatest fencing competition — a sobriquet given by the sport's international governing body. A young Korean fencer provided the biggest highlight.

Above: Korean Kim Young-Ho scores an upset win in the foil over world No.2 Ralf Bissdorf of Germany.

Opposite, main picture: The spectacle of fencing in what the international federation has described as the sport's best competition ever.

Opposite, below right: Timea Nagy of Hungary savors her win in the women's epee.

A 29-year-old from Korea who studied his opponents via video and an Italian police officer emerged as the stars of world fencing following a competition described as the best yet by the sport's international federation.

It certainly resulted in more upsets than ever before at top level and Kim Young-Ho's victory in the men's individual foil was the biggest shock of all.

The Korean, ranked No.5 in the world, was not expected to be among the medallists. He was determined, though, not to become a whipping boy for his more fancied European rivals. Young-Ho's devised his tactics by watching hours of videos of his illustrious rivals. He knew everything about their styles.

In the end, that knowledge and his self-belief proved decisive. He became an instant national hero, winning Korea's first-ever fencing gold medal with a 15-14 win over Germany's world No.2, Ralf Bissdorf, in a gripping final.

Earlier in the quarter-finals, Young-Ho had knocked out the shortest priced favorite to win fencing gold in Sydney, Ukrainian Sergiy Golubytsky.

In a sport dominated for a century by competitors from Europe, the Korean's victory is an indication the power base of the sport is slowly but surely shifting.

The all-powerful French fencing team might have won the most medals in the sport at Sydney, but only took home one gold.

Italy, the other powerhouse, won three gold, while Russia also won three. Germany, the only country to supply a full quota of competitors for every discipline, failed to win any gold.

But while the Korean's victory was completely unexpected, ancient fencing rivalries will always get the blood pumping. Such was the case when Italy and France clashed in the final of the men's team epee tournament.

France, which had gone two days without winning a gold, was set to finally stand at the top of the podium leading by two with one round remaining. But Alfredo Rota, a little Italian policeman, stepped on to the piste, after earlier heroics against Korea, when he wiped a three-point deficit to win in overtime.

The final was a similar story, as he erased a two-point deficit against individual epee silver medallist Hugues Obry to force overtime again. Rota then scored a precision hit to win gold for his country with a score of 39-38. Obry slumped to the ground, too devastated to move, while Rota was thrown high into the air by jubilant Italian officials.

When the hysteria had subsided, the bout was described as one of the greatest ever seen at the Olympic Games.

A major surprise was the dethroning of the sport's biggest name, French fencer Laura Flessel-Colovic. The part-time French model stormed into the semi-finals of the women's individual epee event, before being beaten by Hungary's No.3 Timea Nagy 15-14. Nagy went on to win an unlikely gold, while Flessel-Colovic had to settle for bronze.

The Australians weren't expected to last past the morning qualification rounds, but nobody told 38-year-old Melbourne hospital worker, Gerry Adams.

Adams, whose parents were told he was unlikely to live past his 10th birthday after he was born with a hole in his heart, showed all his fighting qualities by finishing 15th in the individual epee event — the best finish by an Australian epee fencer at the Olympic Games. He backed up from that performance two days later to lead the men's epee team into the quarter-finals, where they eventually finished eighth, another best-ever. Australia's top medal fencing hope, Melbourne lawyer Evelyn Halls, blamed her own poor tactics for crashing out of the women's individual epee event, beaten by sometime training partner, Austria's Andrea Rentmeister, 15-14 in overtime in the Round of 32.

JUDO

It seemed nothing could stop the Japanese march to the podium. The triumph of the Asian masters, whipped into gold medal-winning form by rapturous red and white-clad crowds gave few other countries a look in — but Australia still managed to claim its first judo medal in 36 years.

Above: Maria Pekli came through for Australia, defeating Italy's Cinzia Cavazzuti to take bronze in the 57kg class.

Opposite, top: Australia's Rebecca Sullivan (white) locks up Kye Sun Hui of North Korea.

Opposite, below left: Giorgi Vazagashvili (blue) from Georgia looks to have lost the battle in his final 66kg bout with Patrick Van Kalken (Netherlands) but holds on to take the bronze medal.

Opposite, below right: The pint-sized superstar of the judo mat, Japan's Ryoko Tamura takes gold at her third Olympic attempt.

From the shuddering 196kg frame of Valentyn Rusyakov to the wispy skills of Japan's golden girl Ryoko Tamura, judo enthralled Australia in a manner never seen before.

Sydneysiders learned quickly as the roar of European hope and Asian ecstasy crashed around the Sydney Exhibition Centre with greater authority. The enthusiastic response to competition explained more than any rulebook.

Crowd worship ebbed and flowed from the Japanese, to the Koreans, to France's stars and on to the Cubans as the four major powers of the sport tore at each other for supremacy.

It was, however, Japan which once again reaffirmed its position as the world's premier producer of judokas, leaving our shores with no less than four of the 14 gold medals on offer, one more than it achieved in Atlanta.

And it was Tamura, the women's under 48kg champion, who created much of the Japanese momentum. As the short strides of the pocket judoka carried her on to the mat for her gold medal bout, the venue was a sea of red and white.

Admirers dressed in matching uniforms chanted incantations, all in a bid to carry their hero onward to the medal for which she has so long lusted.

This was, in fact, Tamura's third attempt at Olympic gold, after finishing with silver in 1992 as a 16-year-old behind French star Cecile Nowak and her shock loss to North Korea's Kye Sun Hui in the final at Atlanta. To the sheer delight of her rabid supporters, it was sweet success.

Just two minutes after Tamura's triumph, countryman Tadahiro Nomura added to the euphoria. Nomura's defence of his Olympic crown was spectacular — pinning his rival to the mat 14 seconds into the bout.

While the Japanese influence was felt all around the venue, it was the effort of Australia's Maria Pekli which for many provided a greater highlight. Pekli's performance in the women's under 57kg class left an indelible mark in the memories of those who were fortunate enough to see her compete.

The tenacious 26-year-old kept the home crowd spellbound as she skipped from one round to the next, defying powerhouse nations and lifting the first medal for this country in judo since 1964.

Pekli's bronze was the highlight of an outstanding meet for the Australian team that also finished with two ninth placings, to Daniel Kelly in the men's under 81kg and Rebecca Sullivan in the women's under 52kg.

In his first Olympic Games, Kelly accounted for Barcelona silver medallist Jason Morris and shapes as a leader of Australia's push in coming years.

The emotions of Australia's Robert Ball, though, were locked somewhere between horror and utter surprise.

For four years he had prepared for his Olympic moment and it passed him before he realised. Ball graced the mat for six seconds before he was pinned down — denied the opportunity to exhibit some of the skills that have carried him to success in recent years. Men's coach, Stephen Hill, was just as mystified at Ball's exit at the hands of Adbullo Tangriev of Uzbekistan. "That can happen in judo," Hill said. "He (Tangriev) probably went out on the mat with the preconceived plan of going straight in there and throwing him. Most people don't go for it, but he obviously did."

Ball, 35, had never challenged Tangriev before. "I think I built up more sweat warming up," Ball said. "My mind was just not on the job."

But it was a superb week for Australia; in Atlanta, the entire team managed just two bout wins.

France and Cuba will take much out of this Games, their continual presence in the medal rounds was hard to miss, but both nations still have ground to make up on the Japanese. While Tamura and Nomura will be 29 and 30 when Athens arrives, the next generation of Japanese champions have already emerged.

Kosei Inoue's performance to "own" the men's under 100kg division was unparalleled and, with him at the forefront, Japan looks set to continue its dominance.

TABLE TENNIS

Just who can match it with China? The Asian giants came, saw and conquered at Sydney 2000, winning all four gold medals. The signs are, though, that the rest of the world is trying to work together to end the Chinese reign in future Olympic Games.

Above: Delighted to be sharing the doubles gold medal, China's Wang Nan and Li Ju were adversaries in the women's singles, Wang taking the honors.

Opposite page, top: Wang and Li together in action as the Chinese domination continued.

Opposite page, bottom: Men's singles winner Kong Linghui was top seed and never seriously threatened.

Perennial champion China may have dominated yet again, winning all four gold medals on offer, but the Sydney 2000 Olympic Games will also be remembered as the time Australia finally earned respect on the international stage.

Thought to be cannon-fodder for the stronger Asian and European competitors, the evidence of Australia's improvement could not be disputed.

The host nation thrived on the overwhelming hometown support to win seven matches — six more than in Atlanta.

The stars were Shirley Zhou and Miao Miao, two women brought together last year with a specific eye on Sydney. They didn't disappoint — even attracting the world's richest man, American software guru Bill Gates, to watch one of their matches.

In making the quarter-finals of the doubles, Zhou and Miao went where no other Australians had gone before. Just making the last 16 was a record in itself, but their win over seventh-seeds Ni Xia Lian and Peggy Regenwetter proved it was no fluke.

They succumbed to the power of China's eventual silver medallists Sun Jin and Yang Ying the next evening, but that didn't stop the waving of Australian flags and a stirring rendition of *Waltzing Matilda* from the capacity crowd in recognition of their achievement.

But there were other heroes for Australia. Mark Smythe, ranked 287th in the world, scored the best win of his career when he knocked over Hong Kong's Leung Chu Yan — ranked 229 places higher.

More accustomed to playing before family and friends, the crowd support at the State Sports Centre amazed the Australians. Smythe even credited his win over Leung to the vocal support from the grandstand.

"I think it's the first game I've played where I could say the crowd has won it for me," said the man they call "Duck". "I think he got quite nervous out there — the situation got to him more than it did me."

For all Australia's improvement, Sydney 2000 belonged to China.

Not only did the Chinese win all four gold medals, but they also took three silver and a bronze. Three of the four finals were all-China affairs, with the trend interrupted only by

Sweden's 1992 gold medallist Jan-Ove Waldner in the men's singles.

But after an exciting five games, even he could not repel the Chinese tide as top seed Kong Linghui made it a clean sweep for the heavyweights of the sport.

The golds went to Kong (men's singles), Wang Nan (women's singles), Wang Liqin-Yan Sen (men's doubles) and WangNan-Li Ju (women's doubles).

The medal harvest gives China the remarkable record of 14 golds from a possible 16 since table tennis was introduced to the Olympic Games at Seoul in 1988. The best performance belonged to women's world No.1 Wang, who won gold in both singles and doubles.

To win the singles, Wang had to beat compatriot Li — her partner just 48 hours earlier when they took gold in the doubles.

Liu Gouliang, the first man to win gold in singles and doubles in Atlanta, had to be content with a silver (doubles) and bronze (singles), indicative of the incredible depth of the Chinese team.

The question on the lips of most after the Games was how can anyone catch China?

Before travelling to Sydney, the top European players put aside personal rivalries and held a training camp together in an attempt to thwart the might of the Chinese.

It didn't work.

The only Europeans to win medals were France's Jean-Phillipe Gatien and Patrick Chila (men's doubles) and Sweden's Waldner (men's singles).

But Gatien said the Europeans must continue to work together if China's reign is to be ended.

"Such a camp is a good idea for the future of European players," the Frenchman said. "It is one way we can work towards beating the Chinese.

"They have more young players than us, so their future is rosy. But we must continue to fight on."

For Australia, the players realise their efforts will mean nothing if further progress is not made. In Miao and Zhou, Australia has a doubles pair capable of beating the big guns, while Smythe showed he deserves a higher ranking. Australia's top male player, Simon Gerada, was disappointing and is likely to play in Europe to improve his game.

"If this is a shot in the arm for the sport here then I'm happy," Smythe said of Australia's performance. "I know there are a couple of million who play in the garage, but we need them to go down to the local club. That would do wonders for the sport's future here."

Top: Zhou's partner Miao Miao made her Olympic debut and had a strong impact.

Above: Shirley Zhou has a rosy future in women's doubles after her efforts in Sydney.

Above left: Yen-Shu Chang from Chinese Taipei kept his concentration intact in the men's singles.

Left: Brett Clarke (left) and Jeff Plumb will benefit from their first Olympic experience.

Opposite: The scene at the State Sports Centre, many tables, no waiting.

WEIGHTLIFTING

Women made a spectacular debut in Olympic weightlifting, and there was a changing of the guard among the biggest of the big, the super heavyweights, but the tournament was overshadowed by lifters stripped of medals after several positive drug tests.

Above: China's Ding Meiyuan earned the title of the strongest woman in the world, winning gold in the super heavyweight division.

Opposite page: Akakios Kakiasvilis of Greece completes a lft in the snatch on his way to winning gold in the 94kg division.

Opening spread: The inimitable style of German super heavyweight Ronny Weller.

When the 10 strongest men in the world took the stage at the Darling Harbour convention centre for weightlifting's super heavyweight division, the embattled sport was in desperate need of something special.

These were dark days for weightlifting. The Sydney 2000 Olympic Games had been plagued by drug scandals, moving International Olympic Committee officials to state they would review the sport's future in the Games program.

But there is no doubt weightlifting had its moments of magic and theatre, particularly when the big men took the stage.

Among the super heavyweights were Russian Andrei Chemerkin, the reigning gold medallist who tipped the scales at 174kg, and his long-time rival German Ronny Weller, who took silver in Atlanta.

But this was a competition that would signal the changing of the guard. The sport's biggest and best were set upon by a group of younger lifters, including little known Iranian Hossein Rezazadeh.

What unfolded was considered the greatest weightlifting contest ever. Three world records were broken in the snatch — first by Armenian Ashot Danielyan, then by Weller and finally by Rezazdeh. Meanwhile, Chemerkin was in the mix but 10kg off the pace.

The clean and jerk saw another two world records fall, with Rezazdeh the destroyer. The Iranian finished with a world record combined total of 472.5kg — befitting the title of the world's strongest man.

At just 22, Rezazdeh also became the youngest Olympic super heavyweight champion. His total was the equivalent of lifting five household refrigerators as he beat the most competitive field ever.

Five lifters recorded a total greater than 460kg, an unprecedented result. Chemerkin's gold medal total from Atlanta of 457.5kg would have earned only seventh spot on this night.

Thankfully, the big men put the focus back on the competition because, in the previous two weeks, there had been just as much drama off the lifting platform. Before competition began, two Romanian lifters, Adrian Mateas and Traian Ciherean, returned positive drug

tests in the International Weightlifting Federation's blanket testing. The Romanians were banned, although Mateas denied they were guilty and declared he and his teammate were going on a hunger strike until they were given another drug test. That was not granted. The Romanians had already lost a lifter in May after a positive drug result. Under the IWF's rule, three positive tests for one nation in a calendar year meant Romania either had to pay a US$50,000 fine or be banned from international competition for 12 months. They paid the fine and were allowed to continue but there was little respite from bad news.

Three Bulgarian lifters, all medal-winners, tested positive to a banned diuretic — the first women's gold medallist Izabela Dragneva; Ivan Ivanov who won silver; and

bronze medal winner Sevdalin Minchev. They had all been cleared during the IWF's round of pre-competition testing. There was support for the theory they were using the drug to make their weight division rather than to mask steroids.

All three were stripped of their medals and the Bulgarians were expelled from the games by the IWF without being given an opportunity to pay the fine. IWF vice president, Australian Sam Coffa, admitted the sport had returned to its darkest days of the late 1980s.

Back then, it was Bulgaria that brought the sport into disrepute, expelled from the Seoul 1988 Olympic Games after four athletes, including two medallists, tested positive. Despite the IWF's efforts to clean up the weightlifting community, it was clear there was still much work to be done.

Amid all this there was a continuous stream of drama unfolding back on the stage. Turkey's "little dynamo" Halil Mutlu broke three world records on his way to winning his second gold medal in the lightest of the men's competition, the 56kg division. His triumph was followed by the shock of his teammate, and the greatest weightlifter in history, Naim Suleymanoglu, bowing out of competition without registering a total (lifters must make one successful attempt in the snatch if they are to complete the contest). Suleymanoglu, who weighs just 62kg, was the only lifter to have won three consecutive gold medals before Sydney and had come out of retirement in his pursuit of a record fourth gold — but it was too much for him.

Not so for the golden Greeks, Pyrros Dimas and Akakios Kakiasvilis, who each

Right: A tiny man at just 150cm, but a giant of the sport, Turkey's Halil Mutlu broke three world records on his way to winning the 56kg class, his second Olympic gold medal.

Opposite page, top: Doing it the hard way. Cuban Michael Batista employs an unconventional technique in the men's 94kg snatch.

Opposite page, middle: Turkish superstar Naim Suleymanoglu came out of retirement after three successive gold medals to compete in Sydney but, to the disappointment of the huge crowd, failed to complete a lift in the 62kg class.

Opposite page, below: The strain is just too much. Japan's Mari Nakaga, competing in the 53kg class, topples under the bar.

won their third consecutive gold medals to join Suleymanoglu as greats of the sport.

Women made their Olympic debut, 13 years after their first world championships. Their entry proved to be a study in contrasts: 16-year-old Dika Toua from Papua New Guinea was the first female to lift a weight on the five-ring platform, and she was followed by a 43-year-old mother of four, Brazil's Maria Jorge. The first gold medal for women had gone to Dragneva before being handed down to American Tara Nott. But, as expected, the Chinese dominated the women's events. Their four lifters all won gold and smashed world records. The highlight was, again, the super heavyweights, with China's Ding Meiyuan earning the title of the strongest woman in the world, edging out Poland's Agata Wrobel for gold.

The Australians fared admirably in competition but only former Armenian Sergo Chakhoyan was ever in contention for a medal. Chakhoyan was running third after the snatch in the 85kg division before dropping back. There was a lot of potential on show in the Australian team. Nineteen-year-old Queenslander Amanda Phillips finished sixth in the 63kg division while 20-year-old Anthony Martin broke two Australian records in the B group of the super heavyweights, in the process becoming the first Aboriginal to represent Australia in weightlifting. The Games mark the retirement of veteran lifter Yurik Sarkisian, who won a silver medal for Russia at the Moscow Games in 1980.

Team manager Robert Kabbas said he was pleased with the overall performance of the squad. "In any team where you are not realistically competing for medals, the real measure is personal bests and we can take a lot out of the Games," he said. "We also broke four Commonwealth records and six Australian records. You can't ask for much more than that."

Left: Australia's Amanda Phillips put her heart, soul – and tongue into a lift in the 63kg clean and jerk.

Top: Hossein Rezazadeh, of Iran shares his gold medal podium with German silver medallist Ronny Weller and Armenia's Ashot Danielyan (bronze).

Above: Mexico's Soraya Jimenez celebrates a gold medal in the 58kg division.

Opposite page, top: Latvian super heavyweight Raimonos Bergmanis ends his Olympic campaign after his first attempt at the snatch, dislocating his shoulder.

Opposite page, below: New world record holder Hossein Rezazadeh gives thanks for gold.

BASEBALL

Bigger than the world series? Tommy Lasorda thinks America's first gold medal in Olympic baseball is the sport's ultimate prize and who would argue with a Major League Hall of Famer? Team USA finally broke the Cuban stranglehold on international baseball, while Australia was left to rue missed opportunities.

Above: The absorbing final between USA and Cuba, in which Cuba's extraordinary international run came to an end.

Opposite page: Party time. America claims its "birthright" – an Olympic baseball gold medal.

Opening spread: Fast ball. The unusual pitching style of Japan's Shunsuke Watanabe wowed fans at Blacktown.

When American pitcher Ben Sheets fell to his knees and cast his weary arms to the heavens at 10.04pm on September 27, the jam-packed Baseball Stadium at Sydney Olympic Park erupted in star-spangled splendor.

Sheets, a good ol' boy from America's deep south, had shut-out the powerful Cubans 4-0 to finally secure the gold medal and take it back to baseball's spiritual home.

The significance of the victory was immense in the US where baseball is the "national pastime", given the Cubans had dominated at international level for almost 40 years.

Cuba, a sports-mad island of 11 million people with a production line of world-class baseballers, had won the two previous Olympic gold medals at Barcelona and Atlanta, and 23 of the 25 official world championships since 1939.

But the Cuban empire crumbled in Sydney where an American team of hard-nosed professionals — a combination of journeymen and prospects under legendary manager Tommy Lasorda — outgunned the Cubans in the final.

Lasorda, a Major League Hall of Famer who celebrated his 73rd birthday during the Olympic Games, shed tears as he described "the greatest moment of my life".

"We were the underdogs but everyone in the world will know about these players after tonight," he said. "This is bigger than winning the World Series. I have never been as proud as I was tonight. These guys will carry the torch for others to follow."

The US were beaten 6-1 by Cuba three days before the final but refused to be intimidated by vaunted hitters Omar Linares, Orestes Kindelan and Antonio Pecheco, all members of the gold medal teams at Barcelona and Atlanta. The Americans confronted, and conquered, the might of Cuban pitching in the final when Pedro Luis Lazo, Jose Ibar and the 160kmh fastballs of Maels Rodriguez were handled and dispatched by the US hitters.

Lasorda wisely called on his senior players for input. Catcher Pat Borders, the Most Valuable Player from the Toronto Blue Jays 1992 World Series triumph, outfielders Ernie Young and Mike Neill and third baseman Mike Kinkade played important roles in the campaign. Big-hitting Doug Mientkiewicz hit two game-winning home runs to sink Korea en route to the gold medal playoff.

Mientkiewicz's grand-slam homer in the eighth inning broke a scoreless deadlock in the preliminary round game, then a solo home run at the bottom of the ninth beat Korea 3-2 in a dramatic semi-final.

The crowd-pleasing Koreans, supported by thousands of animated countrymen, deservedly won the bronze medal with a 3-2 defeat of arch-rivals Japan.

For the baseball purist, this was an engrossing encounter with the tenacious Koreans scoring three runs in the eighth inning to win their first Olympic medal in the sport. After losing three of the four opening preliminary round games, Korea overcame injuries, bad calls and two last-gasp losses to the US to claw back to the bronze medal.

The competition was one of the most successful Olympic spectator sports with 245,000 attending games at the Baseball Stadium and 42,000 turning up at Aquilina Reserve, Blacktown. The venues, which drew rave reviews from players, media and fans, were abuzz with action from the opening game when the US beat Japan 4-2 after a marathon 13 innings.

Australia, weakened by the withdrawal or ineligibility of six pitchers in the month prior to the Games, beat Korea 5-3, lost to Cuba 1-0 and stretched Japan before going down 7-3.

But the Australians disappointed against the lesser teams, losing to the Netherlands (6-4) and Italy (8-7) in results which relegated them to seventh place.

"We just didn't play well and failed to get any momentum going," Australian catcher and Major League star David Nilsson said.

"We finished seventh and that was indicative of how we performed."

Despite the dismal finish which failed to capitalise on Australia's win in last year's Intercontinental Cup, Nilsson lived-up to his Major League reputation by easily leading the Olympic batting averages on .565. The only other Australians to hit better than .300 were utility Brett Roneberg and outfielder Grant McDonald. The depleted pitching roster struggled, with only relievers Craig Anderson and Michael Nakamura enhancing their reputations, while starter Shayne Bennett did a fine job against Cuba.

The Netherlands, fielding four players with Major League experience, produced the biggest upset when they ended Cuba's Olympic streak of 21 wins with a stunning 4-2 win in an early game. Cuba's vulnerability in the new Olympic baseball age of professionalism had finally been exposed and was later ruthlessly exploited by an American team intent on claiming what it believes is its birthright.

Above: Too fast, even for the camera. Australia's Paul Gonzales goes after a juicy Japanese pitch.
Left: The desperate dive, Soo-Keun Jung of Korea tries to catch out a Japanese fly ball.

Opposite page, top left: Good ol' boy, Ben Sheets pitches for gold.
Opposite page, middle: Japanese catcher Abe Shinnosuke gives nothing away behind his reflector sunglasses.
Opposite page, bottom left: Even a broken bat couldn't stop Dave Nilsson topping the averages.
Opposite, main picture: Japan's Fumihiro Suzuki can't stop Korean Jong-Ho Park stealing home.

Previous spread: Australia's Grant McDonald pole-axes Korean catcher Kyung-Oan Park, who broke his ribs in the crash.

WORDS | JIM TUCKER

ROWING

The Olympic rowing regatta was dominated by the ascent into legend of British great, Steve Redgrave, who claimed his fifth consecutive gold medal. Australia qualified the most number of boats into the finals, but had to be content with many minor medals.

Above: So what's the fuss? British rowing legend Steve Redgrave demonstrates the stiff upper lip on the victory dais, while James Cracknell can't control his emotions at a gold medal.

Opposite page: The moment of triumph, Tim Foster embraces Redgrave after taking out the men's coxless fours, giving Redgrave a fifth consecutive gold medal. Matthew Pinset and James Cracknell are the other two members of the team.

The golden high five from British marvel Steve Redgrave put the definitive stamp on an Olympic rowing regatta in which the expectations of a record Australian medal assault were never quite met.

The streak Redgrave began in Los Angeles in 1984 reached a remarkable climax when the 38-year-old Brit nailed gold at a fifth consecutive Olympic Games, with an imposing role beside Matthew Pinsent, Tim Foster and James Cracknell in the men's coxless four.

Australian bronze medallist Bo Hanson summed up the admiration for Redgrave, when he put him on the same Olympic pedestal as track and field legend Carl Lewis.

"It's just phenomenal what Steve has done," Hanson said. "Most athletes dream of one gold medal as the pinnacle. I don't think we'll ever see this (five golds) again." It was a generous tribute to the greatest oarsman the sport has known.

The full-house of more than 22,000 on the first day of the rowing finals had seen nothing like the celebrations either. Pinsent, his partner in the pairs for two previous Olympic gold medals, clambered from his place in the boat to embrace Redgrave. A nudge from Redgrave gave him a dunking as sweet as any spray of champagne.

Redgrave didn't wish to nominate the best of his gold medal efforts, yet his crewmates all knew how much extra he needed to drag out for this one. The oarsman has staged a three-year battle to stay on top of life as an insulin-dependent diabetic.

"I think your first Olympic gold medal is probably the best because you have a dream to try and achieve something and it's that dream coming alive," Redgrave said. "Because it's about getting it right one day, every four years, each Olympics is very, very special. It'd be wrong to say which is your best. Like picking a favorite child, you just can't do that."

Redgrave inspired the passions of the crowd at Penrith. One fan swam a Union Jack to the British boat in tribute. More took a dip in the golden pond as the crew cruised a slow victory lap past the massive grandstands that stretched over the final 450m of the course.

The same spontaneous reaction would surely have followed any Australian gold medal performance but it never came. No country matched the host nation's 10 boats into finals yet the No.1 rowing power from 1996 in Atlanta had to settle for three silver and two

bronze. It was like a frustrating AFL scoreline — no goals, five behinds.

While only the Germans, with six, finished with more medals, the 14 golds were split nine ways elsewhere. The powerful Romanians took three and German women's crews had two. The British and French men also claimed two gold.

Tasmania's "Mighty Lighties", Simon Burgess, Anthony Edwards, Rob Richards and Darren Balmforth, gave it the biggest shot for Australia, leading all the way before a moment of agony.

They were overhauled in the final 100m by the French in the lightweight men's coxless four.

The in-form Australian men's eight of Jaime Fernandez, Mike McKay, Rob Jahrling, Alastair Gordon, Daniel Burke, Stuart Welch, Nick Porzig, Christian Ryan and coxswain Brett Hayman started favorites yet blew the start and trailed fifth. Even after they found a motor to pick up nearly three seconds on the British over the final 500m, they were left numb as silver medallists.

The men's and women's eights both installed four speakers rather than three inside their boats so their coxswain's calls could be heard above the roars of the home fans. Hayman resorted to banging the side of the boat, whipping it like a jockey to urge a final, extra effort.

Two years ago, 1996 Olympic gold medallist Kate Slatter peered beneath the eyebrow stud, blue nail polish and crashing music tastes of Rachael Taylor to find a partner who could put her in the hunt for a second Games title. They won a strong silver in the women's pair and Slatter later announced that effort had been her Olympic swansong.

Celebrated two-time gold medallist James Tomkins and Matthew Long had been thrown together by fate little more than two months before the Games. That alone made their late surge for bronze an achievement, yet they knew it was a scratchy row and below their aim. Winners Michel Andrieux and Jean-Christophe Rolland broke a 48-year gold medal drought in rowing for France, ensuring instant hero status.

Twins Geoff and James Stewart celebrated in the crush at Circular Quay on that heady night in 1993 when Sydney won its host city bid, so the bronze they shared with Hanson and Ben Dodwell in the four was

Above: Coxless pair silver medallists Sebastian Bea and Ted Murphy from the USA dive into the crowd to celebrate with fans.

the culmination of a seven-year quest.

Lightweight double scullers Virginia Lee and Sally Newmarch managed fourth as did the men's quad scull of Peter Hardcastle, Stuart Reside, Duncan Free and Jason Day, for their large "Oz Quad Cheer Squad".

World champion Bruce Hick, with partner Haimish Karrasch, was rowed out in the semi-finals in a disappointing end to his career in the lightweight double sculls, while the close-knit Australian women's eight of Victoria Roberts, Alison Davies, Jodi Winter, Bronwyn Thompson, Rachael Kininmonth, Kristina Larsen, Emily Martin, Jane Robinson and coxswain Katie Foulkes were a tearful fifth.

Lee's mother had provided one of the

classic lines in the build-up: "As long as you do your best dear ... you know if it hurts too much you can always stop." It was no motto for single sculler Ekaterina Karsten, of Belarus, who found an incredible second surge to pip Bulgaria's heartbroken Rumyana Neykova by 12/1000ths of a second, or four millimetres, for the gold.

The photo finish took more than 20 minutes to settle, so few begrudged the silver medallist's husband and coach Svilen Neykov the formal protest he later lodged.

Rob Waddell in the men's single scull was a far more commanding victor as New Zealand's gold medal drought-breaker. Romanian policewoman Elisabeta Lipa won her fourth Olympic gold, this time in the

women's eight, and vowed she would row on to Athens in 2004 in her attempt to match Redgrave's five golds.

The seven Chinese rowers dropped from their Olympic team for irregular blood index levels never reached the regatta and the positive test for nandrolone that stained Latvian sculler Andris Reinholds was shunted into the background by the performances on the water.

The blustery winds feared by organisers never arrived and the conditions were near-perfect throughout.

Leading Australian coach Brian Richardson was left to sum up the team's feelings about missing gold:

"Maybe, we wanted to do it too much."

Above: Kate Slatter and Rachael Taylor took to the water to show off their silver medals in the women's coxless pairs. Slatter, an Atlanta gold medallist, later announced her retirement.

Left: Matthew and Luke Taylor swam out to make sure sister Rachael knew she was a silver medallist.

Above: Sunset on another spectacular day of

Top left: James Tomkins and Matt Long gave their all to claim bronze in the coxless pairs.

Above: It was France's turn to fly the flag at Penrith, as Tomkins and Long look on during the coxless pairs medal ceremony.

Middle, left: Slovenia's Iztok Cop and Luka Spik in action in the final of the men's double sculls.

Left: An opportunity missed – lightweight double sculls pair Haimish Karrasch and Bruce Hick reflect on what might have been, after finishing seventh.

Top: A slow start cost the men's eight dearly, coming home like a steam train to be pipped by the British crew.

Above: Australia's "Mighty Lighties", the men's lightweight coxless four, get ready to receive their silver medals, from left Simon Burgess, Anthony Edwards, Darren Balmforth and Robert Richards.

Left: The Romanians had a hugely successful regatta, this time celebrating victory in the women's eights.

Opposite, top left and right: The feats of Steve Redgrave and his coxless four team inspired huge loyalty among British fans, who braved the cold water at Penrith Lakes to celebrate with their oarsmen.

Opposite, middle: Australia's Georgina Douglas enjoys a moment of quiet reflection, preparing for the single sculls.

Opposite, below left: Olympic debutants James and Geoff Stewart show off their matching bronze medals.

Opposite, below right: The Stewarts joined Bo Hanson and Ben Dodwell in the coxless fours, where they attempted to win Australia's third successive gold in the event.

FOOTBALL

WORDS | DAVE LEWIS

FOOTBALL

The world game became a highlight of the Olympic Games when two unheralded nations upset football's fancied teams to claim the men's and women's gold. For Australia's Olyroos and Matildas, though, it was yet again a case of too many opportunities missed.

Above: Cameroon football players celebrate their first Olympic gold medal.

Opposite page: The winning goal. Cameroon's Pierre Wome slips a penalty past Spanish goalkeeper Aranzubia to clinch the game 5-3 on penalties.

Opening spread: Football started the Sydney 2000 Olympic Games with a superb ceremony at the Melbourne Cricket Ground.

Football was the games within the Games — 48 matches attended by over one million converts in five cities and shock winners in both the men's and women's competitions.

Australians might not be born and bred followers of the world's most popular sporting code but if the Olympic Games proved anything, it showed when the marquee acts come to town, people want to watch them.

The ailing National Soccer League is one thing, this was something else entirely.

Even after the suffocating disappointment of early exits by the self-destructive Olyroos and misfiring Matildas, the hordes continued to pour through the gates in Melbourne, Adelaide, Brisbane, Sydney and Canberra.

A sport often derided for its lack of goals churned out an average of over four per game.

The drama was drip-fed as both the men's and women's draws painted a palate of vivid excitement, melded with joy and heartbreak.

African champions Cameroon, the people's choice against Spain in the men's final, were consecrated as gold medallists in a penalty shootout spectacular which highlighted soccer's shifting sands.

Once again, the new world triumphed over the established order.

Played in front of 98,000 at the Olympic Stadium, the match squeezed every drop of emotion from audience and combatants alike with spectacular goals, disallowed goals, glaring misses, two red cards, a momentous fightback by the Africans and the theatre of a shootout.

The women's final between the star spangled glamor girls of USA, the World Cup champions, and unfashionable Norway was no less absorbing.

The world number one Americans equalised eight seconds from the end to tie the match up at 2-2, only to be beaten by a dramatic golden goal as the game went into extra time.

Such was the climax, but the foreplay was never dull either as football put on its boldest face and strutted out as the life of the party.

The crowning of Cameroon underlined Africa's emergence as a genuine threat to the game's status quo.

Just as Nigeria managed to do against Argentina in the final at Atlanta four years ago, Cameroon came from behind to gore Spain after trailing 2-0 at half-time.

It may have taken a 5-3 penalty shootout margin to achieve it, but the Spaniards should have been banished long before it got to that stage.

Six of coach Jean-Paul Akons' sublime young team are already regulars in the country's senior side.

The next phase of their rapid evolution should be at the 2002 World Cup where their intimidating physical presence, technical attributes and sheer artistry could see them become the first African country to win the game's paramount prize.

However Akons has yet to be convinced the African revolution is about to knock monoliths like Italy, Brazil and France from soccer's summit.

"The Olympic tournament is designed for players who are under 23 and while it's a major achievement for any country to win gold, it doesn't mean a World Cup is necessarily next," he mused.

"Africa is still a long way behind Europe in terms of organisation and finance at all levels of the game.

"We have a lot of work to do yet before we can win a World Cup."

Africa was once derided as a continent full of teams whose players knew how to attack but had the defensive instincts of the Keystone Cops.

Cameroon, still remembered for reaching the quarter finals of the World Cup in 1990, have put that stereotype to rest.

Now it's the Australians, both men and women, who must shatter some stereotypes of their own if they are to be taken seriously as a world power in waiting.

Their penchant for snatching defeat from the jaws of draws — or even victory — saw the Olyroos lose all three group games by the odd goal.

The spectacle evoked comparisons with the heart-rending World Cup qualifying loss to Iran in 1997 at the Melbourne Cricket Ground.

Defensive laspes and the absence of headline act Harry Kewell, who succumbed to injury before the tournament, were decisive as an expectant nation was yet again let down. Tears flowed after the decisive loss to Nigeria and more may yet come when the sport's administrators consider the future of the team.

The Matildas displayed the same suicidal tendencies as the men, squandering the chance to reach the semi-finals by tossing away a 1-0 lead against Brazil with two dreadful errors.

Opposite, top left: Hayden Foxe couldn't control his emotions as the Olyroo campaign ended against NIgeria.

Opposite, top right: Cameroon and Spain could not be separated during normal play and extra time. The Africans held their nerve during a penalty shoot-out to win. It was the second successive time an African nation had won the men's gold.

Opposite, bottom left: Australia struggled vainly against 1996 champions Nigeria, going down 3-2.

Opposite bottom right: Mark Viduka cut an elegant figure in attack against Italy.

Above: Norway's Dangy Mellgren celebrates the goal that won gold 3-2 over the highly-fancied USA.

Below: Australia's Sunni Hughes celebrates a goal against the mighty Brazilians.

WORDS | LEO SCHLINK

CYCLING

Australia's first gold on the track in 16 years was emotion-charged, and a fitting farewell for national coach Charlie Walsh. But cycling crowned a new queen at the Sydney 2000 Olympic Games — Dutchwoman Leontien Zijlaard won three gold, one on the track and both women's road races.

Above: Leontien Zijlaard claimed her third gold of the Games with an emphatic win on the road in the women's time trial.

Opposite page: There wasn't a dry eye at Dunc Gray Velodrome when Scott McGrory and Brett Aitken won the madison.

Opening spread: Powering for the finish line. The road races were a blaze of color.

Seldom has the austere world of international track cycling been so saturated with emotion, drama and brilliance. Australia had waited 16 years, and to the last evening of the Olympic track program, before South Australian Brett Aitken and Victorian Scott McGrory delivered the drought-breaking gold medal, which also served as national coach Charlie Walsh's gilt-edged farewell.

Pitted against the world's finest madison combinations, Aitken and McGrory celebrated not just for themselves and Australia, but for family members, both lost and stricken. As McGrory held his arms aloft in unrestrained joy, having narrowly avoided a last-lap crash, he thought of the three-month-old baby son he and his partner Donna had farewelled in June when Alexander Scott McGrory died after a heart illness. And Aitken, riding at his last Games, had been inspired by the pre-race smiles of two-year daughter Ashli, who suffers from Rhett's syndrome, which restricts limb movement. It seemed everybody at Dunc Gray velodrome was on familiar terms with the veteran pair, triggering a flood of tears and a tidal wave of patriotism. Aitken and McGrory had the gold medals they could only have dared covet. It was Australia's sole cycling gold and left Walsh with two gold, nine silver and nine bronze medals to show for his 20-year reign, a span marred by the ugly explosion of drug cheats and mishaps.

As ever, France was to the fore with the incomparable Felicia Ballanger dominating the 500m time trial, again pushing Michelle Ferris into the silver medal position, and also the blue-riband sprint where she was taken to a third and deciding race by Oxana Grichina. Russian Grinchina will forever rue an ill-contrived stalling manouevre on the bell lap, shuddering to a halt as the French champion slid underneath to quickly build an unassailable lead. Florian Rousseau plundered the keirin gold medal, driving to the line to edge Victorian veteran Gary Neiwand out of a deserved gold medal in a photo-finish. Neiwand, a bronze medallist in Seoul and a silver medallist in Barcelona, had been the architect of Australia's bronze medal in the Olympic Sprint at these Games. The oldest man in the bullish sprint fraternity, 34-year-old Neiwand showcased his staggering talents each time he slipped into the saddle in the three-rider Olympic sprint, effectively masking the

sluggishness of Darryn Hill and debutant Sean Eadie's tardy starts.

France won the Olympic sprint final from Games revelation Great Britain, for whom the dated international concept of financial support for athletes and a centralised training base have been 21st century discoveries. The British produced the most stunning upset at the track with journeyman Jason Queally's triumph in the 1000m time trial, the event swamped with focus on world champion Arnaud Tournant, of France, and Victorian Shane Kelly.

Kelly overcame the horror of his pedal pull in Atlanta by claiming the bronze behind Queally, who rode almost three seconds inside his previous best time, and German stalwart Stefan Nimke.

Germany's outstanding endurance performer Robert Bartko twice rode his way into history at Bankstown, first as winner of

the 4000m individual time trial (where he beat compatriot Jens Lehmann) and then as part of the first team to ride under four minutes — 3:59.710.

In smashing what had been considered an impenetrable barrier, Bartko joined with Lehmann, Guido Fulst and Daniel Becke to destroy Ukraine in the final. Great Britain was third after Australia lost to Germany in the quarter-finals in the second-fastest time. The world record fell twice in the event, first to Ukraine and then to Germany.

Brad McGee was an inspiration in the individual pursuit, snaring the bronze medal after breaking his collarbone two weeks before the Games.

Dutchwoman Leontien Zijlaard was the lead act in women's endurance, and virtually everywhere else, too.

The dusky brunette set a world record in the 3000m individual pursuit and then

easily won the final against France's Marion Clignet. Yvonne McGregor, of Great Britain, was third. Riding an Australian-made bike, Zijlaard threatened to steal the points race but was eventually denied by Italian Antonella Bellutti with Russian Olga Slioussareva third. South Australian Alayna Burns finished seventh.

Spaniard Juan Llaneras rode a typically clever tactical race to land the men's points race from Milton Wynants, of Uruguay, and Russian Alexey Markov, while American enforcer Marty Nothstein deservedly won the sprint from Rousseau and Atlanta and Barcelona gold medallist Jens Fiedler.

As expected, road competition was a highlight for cycling purists. Never before had Australia played host to such an impressive collection of talent. Fittingly, Zijlaard prevailed in a 119km road race dominated by foul weather over fellow stars

Hanka Kupfernagel, of Germany, and Lithuanian Diana Ziliute. Australian favorite Anna Wilson was fourth in a desperate finish.

German gun Jan Ullrich won the men's event over 239km in brutal heat and humidity, savaging the most accomplished field ever assembled in Australia with a nine-second win over Deutsche Telekom team-mates Alexandre Vinokourov, of Kazakhstan, and German Andreas Kloeden. Lance Armstrong was 13th and Marco Pantani 69th. Robbie McEwen was the leading Australian in 19th place.

Zijlaard returned to the road course on the final Saturday to obliterate a class field, winning the 31.2km time trial by 37 seconds from American Mari Holden and French veteran Jeannie Longo-Ciprelli. The unlucky Anna Wilson was again fourth.

Russian Viacheslav Ekimov, gold medallist in the team's pursuit in Seoul 12 years ago, upstaged a celebrated field to win the men's time trial from Ullrich and Armstrong. Queeslander Nathan O'Neill finished a brave 19th after falling on the first lap.

The first mountain bike medal competition delivered mixed results for Australia. Gold medal favorites Mary Grigson (sixth) and Cadel Evans (seventh) both performed creditably but were upstaged by phenomenal performances by Italian Paola Pezza and Frenchman Miguel Martinez respectively.

Pezza secured a controversial victory after a contentious collision with Spaniard Margarita Fullana, who finished third. Swiss Barbara Blatter was second. Grigson's team-mate Alison Baylis finished 21st, paving the way for a gripping men's race.

Swiss veteran Thomas Frischknecht's breakneck speed in the heat, dust and danger was thought to be the perfect prelude for a golden finish, but he was ovewhelmed by the extraordinary speed, stamina and skill of diminutive Martinez, his arch-rival.

Above: The huge field in the 239km men's road race battled brutal heat and humidity.

Left: Australia's Robbie McEwen makes his move at the head of the pack.

Opposite page, top: Leontien Zijlaard had no peers in the road or the track, winning her third gold medal of these Games in the women's time trial.

Opposite page, bottom left: Men's time trial winner Viacheslav Ekimov of Russia also won gold in the teams pursuit in Seoul in 1988.

Opposite page, bottom right: Men's road race gold medallist and frequent Australian visitor, Jan Ullrich of Germany.

Above: The streets of Bronte, in Sydney's eastern suburbs, were plastered with messages for the riders in the women's road event, particularly Australian favorite Anna Wilson.

Right: It was yet another Dutch triumph, Leontien Zijlaard stayed ahead of the pack to claim victory in the 119km road race. Anna Wilson was narrowly beaten out of a bronze medal.

Above: A demanding course awaited the mountain bike fields at Fairfield City Farm. Australia's Cadel Evans struggled valiantly to come in seventh.

Below left: Too steep. Corine Dorland of the Netherlands carries her bike down this part of the mountain bike course.

Below middle: To the winner, the celebration. Miguel Martinez of France was a convincing winner of the men's mountain bike, The field had to dodge snakes, lizards and magpies during the race.

Below right: Controversial winner of the women's race, Italy's Paola Pezzo gets up close and personal with one of the local inhabitants after receiving her gold medal. Pezzo was involved in a contentious crash with Spain's Margarita Fullana.

Above: Scott McGrory (left) and Brett Aitken immediately rode to their families to give thanks for an emotional victory in the madison, a discipline which made its Olympic debut.

Right: McGrory and Aitken's winning style. One rider sprints at any one time and "slings" his partner into the action to share the workload.

Above: In the team pursuit final, the Germans broke what had been considered an impenetrable barrier, the first team to ride under four minutes.

Far left: The incomparable French track champion, Felicia Ballanger, blew away all opposition.

Left: Veteran Gary Neiwand was forced into silver in the final sprint of the keirin.

Above: No mistakes this time. Shane Kelly was a picture of concentration in the 1000m time trial.

Left: Beaten by French great Felicia Ballanger, the final rider of the 500m time trial, Australia's Michelle Ferris rode straight to her family to celebrate a silver medal.

Opposite, top: The strain shows on the faces of Australia's Sean Eadie and German Jan Van Eijden in the Olympic sprint.

Opposite, below left: Darryn Hill celebrates his bronze with a wheelie.

Opposite, below middle: Dutch rider Leontien Zijlaard rode an Australian-designed bike to win the women's individual pursuit.

Opposite, below right: Brad McGee did a patriotic lap of honor after claim bronze in the individual pursuit.

TENNIS

The sentimental journey for Mark Woodforde and Todd Woodbridge didn't have quite the ending Australian fans demanded. The most successful doubles partnership in the history of tennis bowed out of the Olympic Games with silver, Australia's only medal of the tournament.

Above: Tennis diva Venus Williams added an Olympic gold medal to her burgeoning trophy cabinet.

Opposite page: Farewell and thanks. The Woodies fought all the way to finish with silver.

For a duo instinctively aware of the other's next move on the court, Todd Woodbridge and Mark Woodforde strangely didn't know how to react when the curtain dropped for the last time. Woodbridge simply buried his forehead into his partner's shoulder before congratulating opponents Daniel Nestor and Sebastien Lareau on their gold heist that ended a decade of dominance.

"I was just emotional because it was over," Woodbridge said. "I had blocked it out the whole year. We both have got a new beginning, but it was an incredible feeling out there. It felt like we didn't win, but we won anyway."

The Canadians gatecrashed the Woodies' farewell bash; the interlopers who ruined the sentimental script with their 5-7 6-3 6-4 7-6 (7-2) victory in the Olympic men's doubles final that consigned the Australians to silver.

It was the end of a partnership born in August, 1990, that reaped 11 major doubles titles, including each of the four grand slams, two world crowns, a record 61 titles and gold at Atlanta four years earlier — not to mention financial security for the rest of their lives.

Woodforde, who turned 35 during the Games, planned to retire after the Davis Cup final in December and Woodbridge, awaiting the birth of his first child around the same time, will link with Swede Jonas Bjorkman at the start of the new year.

"I wish I could quit now actually," a wistful Woodford said.

"If this could be the last match I had to play ever again, I would be very comfortable with that. Just because it's silver today ... our whole partnership has been gold and it will always be gold and it won't be tarnished."

Despite the enormity of the occasion and crowd support normally reserved for a home Davis Cup tie, the Woodies never really ignited.

Perhaps it was the subconscious reminder there was gold back in the trophy cabinets at home anyway, or a brutal indicator that indeed the most successful doubles team in the history of the game was definitely finished.

While the Woodies are entitled to bask in 10 years of glory, it was an acute awareness of history that drove Russian Yevgeny Kafelnikov relentlessly towards the men's singles gold medal. The 26-year-old from Sochi, a resort on the Black Sea, had his nation's rich Olympic heritage burned into his soul as a boy and he admitted to being in awe of the Soviet stars marching proudly at the opening ceremony. As Russia's tennis flagbearer for years, Kafelnikov had been upstaged by younger teammate Marat Safin's US Open triumph. So, when the still-celebrating Safin stumbled in the first round, it fell to Kafelnikov to pick up the colors. "My confidence was so bad coming in to the Olympics that I was just hoping to participate, you know, to have the record that I was in the Olympics. To win a gold medal is beyond all expectations," Kafelnikov said after outlasting gallant German Tommy Haas 7-6 (7-4) 3-6 6-2 4-6 6-3 in a gold medal match befitting a grand slam final.

It was an underwhelming competiton for the Australian men, but the tournament referee did the host team no favors. Lleyton Hewitt and Pat Rafter lost first round night matches in cold, windy conditions and even Mark Philippoussis' third round with Kafelnikov was after dark. But imagine how prepared Jelena Dokic will be in Athens in 2004. She won four matches to reach the medal rounds, bowing to high-ranked Russian Elena Dementieva with dignity and then succumbed to hungry Monica Seles in the bronze play-off.

American Venus Williams emphasised the chasm between the elite women and the chasing pack by extending her unbeaten streak to 32 matches. The US Open and Wimbledon champion enjoyed a comfortable 6-2 6-4 win over Dementieva in a lopsided women's singles final. Venus need not have been concerned that kid sister Serena would go home empty-handed either. Next day the sisters required just 49 minutes to collect gold, thrashing Kristie Boogert and Miriam Oremans of the Netherlands 6-1 6-1 in the doubles final.

Left: Venus Williams chased down everything to take gold for the USA in singles.

Above: The new force in women's tennis, the Williams sisters, fly the flag for the USA.

Opposite page, top: Pat Rafter lapped up the Olympic experience but it didn't translate into results, bundled out by Canada's Daniel Nestor in the second round.

Opposite page, below left: The Woodies' fairytale ended at the hands of Canadian doubles pair Sebastien Lareau and Daniel Nestor.

Opposite page, below right: Yevgeny Kafelnikov gave all for Mother Russia in the men's singles, confirming his status as Russia's No.1 male player.

WORDS | CATRIONA DIXON AND CARLY CHYNOWETH

SYNCHRONISED SWIMMING

The sheer artistry was breathtaking, but behind the glitter and the glamor, the synchronised swimming competition signalled a massive shift at the top of the sport. The reign of the Americans and Canadians was ended at the hands of mighty Russia.

Above: Ending the North American reign, Olga Brusnikina and Maria Kisseleva celebrate duet gold.

Opposite page, above: In perfect harmony, Mexican sisters Erika and Lillian Leal enter the water in the duet free final.

Opposite page, below: The Russian team on their way to complete dominance of synchro gold.

The end, when it came, was abrupt. North America found itself with nowhere to go when the gold medals were awarded in synchronised swimming.

The United States and Canada have had a mortgage on the major medals since synchro became an Olympic sport in 1984 at Los Angeles, between them winning the seven gold and seven silver medals on offer. But not even this rich tradition could help the former champions tame Russia, which has dominated the world stage since the 1998 world championships.

In Sydney, Russia crowned itself as the premier nation in the sport, winning both the duet and team gold medals. The Russians proved themselves as the most superior athletes in the world in the sport with breathtaking routines in both the technical and free categories. In the duet final, Olga Brusnikina and Maria Kisseleva displayed brilliance, scoring a maximum 65 points for their free routine which, added to 34.580 from the technical routine, gave them an overall score of 99.580 points out of 100. It was as close to perfect as the sport has seen.

It was a victory that earned them a place in Olympic history as the first Russian team to win the synchronised gold. It also came in the wake of a tumultuous year in which the duet were stripped of their European gold medal after Kisseleva failed a drug test for ephedrine.

"Yes, of course this is compensation for the Europeans," Kisseleva said. "It was a great shock and a real tragedy for us in Helsinki. But later we gathered ourselves, used our strength and put everything in place in order to try and win the gold medal.

"There is a real sense of pride for Russia and ourselves. There is a great deal of happiness. We still find it hard to believe this happened."

Japan duet Miya Tachibana and Miho Takeda upset their fancied French opponents Virginie Mengual and Paola Tirados for the silver medal with a score of 98.650 to 97.437.

Despite missing the final, Australian duet Irena Olevsky and Naomi Young achieved the nation's best result in the history of Olympic synchronised swimming, performing in an event which is likely to be their last as a pair.

The hometown couple placed 16th out of 24 teams but their performance still earned

them a place in sporting legend as the first Australian team to qualify for the Games on their own merit.

Although their score of 87.007 didn't meet their own personal expectations, the Games have been a fitting finale for the duet who have struggled financially to compete internationally and train together over the past two years. Uncertain about their future, Olevsky and Young said their performance was an appropriate farewell if they should decide not to continue together after they take a three-month break in the wake of the Games.

The teams event provided Russia with another opportunity to wow the crowd. An exhilarating free routine combined with their high technical marks gave them an overall score of 99.146 points.

DIVING

Australian diving sprang to new heights during the Olympic Games, claiming its first medals since Dick Eve won the plain high dive at Paris in 1924. Once again, though, the springboards and platforms were dominated by another clinical performance from the Chinese.

Above: A superb performance by Xiong Ni of China won him the 3m springboard gold.

Opposite page: Winners are grinners, Australians Dean Pullar and Robert Newbery show off their 3m synchronised bronze.

It had been one of the longest droughts in Australia's sporting history, 76 years without an Olympic diving medal. And when the heavens finally opened above the glistening waters of the Olympic diving pool on Thursday, September 28, it didn't rain, it poured. Within one fine hour, two pairs of Australians soared to bronze medals in the new Olympic discipline of synchronised diving, both finishing behind deserved gold medallists from China.

Not since Dick Eve at Paris in 1924 had Australia won an Olympic diving medal.

It was a case of "ladies first" as Loudy Tourky and Rebecca Gilmore claimed the honor of being the first medallists. They dramatically recovered from seventh after the second round to snatch bronze — Australia's first women's medal in Olympic diving history — with their final dive in the 10m synchronised competition.

For Tourky and Gilmore, being able to bask in the warmth of the 17,000-odd crowd appealed to their sense of irony. In the lead-up to the Games, the two 21-year-olds —Gilmore from Oatlands in NSW, Tourky from Brisbane — were forced to train in freezing conditions at the Olympic pool as the aquatic centre was turned into a construction site to prepare it for competition. Eventually they moved north to Brisbane to complete their build-up.

Pumped up by the women's performance, Australia's men's 3m synchronised team of Dean Pullar and Robert Newbery held off two of the world's strongest diving nations, the US and Mexico, to also come away with the bronze. And they, too, had the odds stacked against them. Pullar, 27, the self-titled "old man" of the Australian team, injured his neck in training the day before the final, the muscles going into painful spasm. When he woke on the day of the final still in agony, he had no choice but to have two painkilling injections.

But there was nothing to dull the emotional pain Newbery took into the final. He knew he had to perform the reverse dive he had botched in the individual competition, costing him what had appeared a certain place in the individual springboard final two days earlier.

Small wonder Australian team manager Val Beddoe, herself an Olympic finalist, came away from the final night of diving at the Games convinced that her squad had turned a corner. The Australians finished with two bronze, a fourth, two fifths, a seventh and an 11th, the nation's best diving result.

The well-drilled Chinese dominated the diving in Sydney, winning five gold and five silver medals in the eight finals.Xiong Ni won the men's 3m springboard event and became the second man after American Greg Louganis to win back-to-back Olympic springboard titles.

It was the closest finish in the men's springboard event for 92 years with Russian great Dmitri Saoutine, the best-known diver in the world, earning bronze. Pullar finished fifth. On the final night of the Olympic diving competition, a bandaged Saoutine put his battered body on the line in the men's individual 10m platform competition but could only manage bronze as Louganis' Olympic platform record was finally consigned to history by Chinese pair Tian Liang and Hu Jia.

Tian, fourth in Atlanta four years ago, claimed the gold with a 724.53 tally that eclipsed Louganis' mark from the 1984 Los Angeles Games by 13.62 points.

In a staggering display of courage he nailed the most difficult dive attempted in the final, a back three-and-a-half somersault, for a perfect 10 to register the first 100-plus dive in Olympic history.

Australia was the best-performed nation in the preliminaries of the men's 10m platform event, but both Mathew Helm and Newbery's dives in the final tailed off a little from the electrifying form they displayed in the earlier rounds. The undoubted highlight was Helm's score of 10 from the Zimbabwean judge for his armstand back double somersault one-and-a-half twister.

Chinese darling Fu Mingxia, a triple Olympian at just 23, joined the ranks of the diving legends as she claimed her fourth gold medal with a successful defence of her women's 3m springboard title.

Only Americans Louganis and Pat McCormick have won as many Olympic diving golds.

Australia's Chantelle Michell finished seventh, the nation's best result in the event since Beddoe finished two places better in Los Angeles in 1984. But China didn't have it all their own way in Sydney.

Saoutine and his partner Igor Loukachine claimed gold in the men's 10m synchronised event while their Russian team-mates Vera Ilina and Ioulia Pakhalina won the women's 3m springboard synchronised event. and Laura Wilkinson, the all-American teenager with a deep faith in God, staged the biggest upset when she seized gold in the women's 10m platform event. The 18-year-old from Houston, Texas, beat favourite Li Na by a point to claim her nation's first gold in the women's Olympic platform event since 1964.

Above: It was all ends up for Great Britain's Tony Ally in the 3m springboard preliminaries. He finished in 12th place.

Right: The beauty of diving happens below the water as well.

Opposite page: Synchronised diving proved a huge hit with fans. America's Jenny Keim and Laura Wilkson looked tangled together off the 10m platform.

Top and Above: Australia's synchronised divers confounded the experts, winning their way through to the bronze in the 3m events.

Right: Russian pair Vera Ilina and Loulia Pakhalina on their way to gold in the synchronised 3m springboard final.

Opposite page: American Laura Wilkinson ended the Chinese dominance from the platform.

SAILING

Local knowledge powered the Australian sailing team to its first Olympic gold medals in 28 years. It was the first time Olympic sailing had been considered a spectator sport, held within the confines of Sydney's world-famous harbor, with masses of vocal fans cheering on their sailors.

Above: The Australian medallists gathered on the steps of the Opera House for their victory ceremonies.

Opposite page: The pressure is off for gold medallists Belinda Stowell and Jenny Armstrong.

Opening spread: Mark Turnbull and Tom King piloting their 470 to a gold medal winning performance.

At an Olympic Games where the sport of sailing underwent a name, image and venue change, history was re-written by a group of relatively unknown Australian athletes, catapulted into the limelight with their record-making feats.

On the world famous Sydney Harbour within sight — and sound — of spectators for the first time in Olympic history, Australian sailors claimed a record haul of four medals from 12 days of sailing.

Pre-regatta predictions of up to nine medals were optimistic, but unrealistic. Australia still bettered its best previous Olympic result of two gold medals, adding a silver and bronze.

The highlight was the gold medal won by the 470 crew of Jenny Armstrong and Belinda Stowell, an achievement acknowledged by unprecedented spectator appreciation.

Harbor traffic stopped to honor the victory — a passenger ferry changing course, its delighted passengers breaking into the "Aussie, Aussie Aussie" victory cry.

Armstrong and Stowell's gold was the first Olympic medal won by female sailors and the 14th overall for the host nation, a feat which marked this Games as Australia's most successful. It also ended sailing's 28-year gold medal drought.

"When we heard that, it made the medal just that extra bit more special — if that is possible," 29-year-old Stowell said.

Thousands of sailing converts thronged to the harbor foreshores for the best "free" ticket in town. The innovation of country codes and colourful national flags on mainsails proved a big hit with spectators able to follow the fortunes of sailors from both land and water.

"The roar from the spectators on the shore watching us was one of the most incredible things I have ever heard," Tornado silver medallist Darren Bundock said. "When we were down it lifted us to new heights.

"Normally we are so far from land no one can see us but this time the crowds on the foreshores had a birds-eye view and I think every sailor here appreciated the fact that for once our sport was firmly in the spotlight."

Just a little over an hour after Armstrong and Stowell collected gold, Australian team-mates Tom King and Mark Turnbull gave Australia its second Olympic victory in the men's 470 class.

In an amazing form reversal, the 27-year-old King went from Australia's worst performed sailor at the Atlanta Games to one of its best just four years later.

With the affable Turnbull as his crew and under the guidance of former Ukraine Victor Kovalenko, the pair dominated the 11-race dinghy competition to secure gold ahead of American rivals Paul Foerster and Bob Merrick.

Just a day later Sydney sport scientist Michael Blackburn sailed to a bronze in the single-handed Laser — a class that produced perhaps the most exciting moment of the Games.

While Blackburn sailed to preserve his bronze, Briton Ben Ainslie and Brazil's Robert Scheidt went head-to-head in a thrilling match-racing battle. Scheidt was later disqualified, handing the 23-year-old Englishman his first gold.

In the first, turbulent week, unseasonally light and shifty breezes blew away the chances of a number of leading Australian contenders, including triple world champion Chris Nicholson and his crew Daniel Phillips in the 49er class and Barcelona bronze medallist Lars Kleppich in the Mistral sailboard.

The lone success that week came via the talented and versatile duo of Bundock and John Forbes.

Hindered by the ultra-light breeze that

played into the hands of their much lighter Austrian rivals Roman Hagara and Hans Pieter Steinacher, Bundock and Forbes fought valiantly to stay in the Tornado medal hunt.

Guided by Sydney's Mike Fletcher, coaching at his seventh Olympic Games, the silver saw the 30-year-old Forbes become only the second Australian to win two Olympic sailing medals, after capturing bronze at Barcelona in 1992.

The leading nation in Olympic classes going into the Games, Australia was forced to hand over the mantle on the final day to the well-funded and well-drilled Great Britain team.

The Brits sailed away with gold in the women's Europe class, the Finns and the Laser racing courtesy of Shirley Robertson, Iain Percy and Ainslie.

They also collected unexpected silvers from 49er sailors Ian Barker and Simon Hiscocks and the Star crew of Ian Walker and Mark Covell.

The British tally of five medals saw it claim the title of top performing sailing nation ahead of Australia with its two gold, silver and bronze.

New Zealand, which finished 11th in the sailing medal count with two sailboard bronze, will also be remembered for claiming a slice of history at the Games.

Veteran sailor Barbara Kendall became the first woman to win a sailing medal at three consecutive Games with her bronze in the Mistral sailboard class — an appropriate result given the Olympic Movement is celebrating 100 years of women's participation in the Games.

At the end of the first Olympic sailing program within the confines of a harbor, 14 nations shared the 33 medals.

And all 404 sailors, in 11 classes and representing 69 nations showed their delight in a unique opportunity to be cheered on by fans from the shore.

Above left: John Forbes took his second Olympic medal, a silver in the Tornado class with crew-mate Darren Bundock.

Middle: Not every day was blue skies and plain sailing. Australian Melanie Dennison and the Europe fleet struggled in heavy weather.

Left: City office workers had the grandstand seats for the 49er fleet racing.

Top: The Europe fleet was the lone women only class in Olympic sailing.

Opposite page: Every shot a picture postcard. The Soling fleet sailed in front of the Sydney Opera House.

Above: One of the most open classes in Olympic sailing, Australia had never seriously threatened the medal positions in the 470 for either men or women before, but the men's and women's teams triumphed, taking gold.

Above: The most vibrant class was undoubtedly the Mistral sailboard. Australians Lars Kleppich and Jessica Crisp did not cope well with the light winds in the first week of competition.

Opposite, top: Michael Blackburn shelved his "bridesmaid" tag, claiming bronze in the Laser class. He finished fourth at both the 1996 Olympic Games and the 1999 world championships.

Opposite, below left: Blackburn's consistent form throughout the regatta was finally rewarded.

Opposite, below right: The three-time world championship-winning crew of Chris Nicholson and Daniel Phillips survived a protracted legal battle to compete at Sydney, but the flukey conditions of the first week did not help their campaign, finding it difficult to recover from a disastrous capsize.

TAEKWONDO

One of two sports making its debut in the Olympic Games, taekwondo provided an unexpected medal rush for Australia. Regarded as the Korean national sport, Australia's exponents had spent much of their lead-up to Sydney learning from the masters.

Above: Medal celebrations for Lauren Burns, with dad Ronnie (top) and Daniel Trenton.

Opposite page: The gold medal winning style of Lauren Burns, comprehensively defeating Cuba's Urbia Melendez Rodriguez.

Lauren Burns and Daniel Trenton did more than win medals at the Sydney 2000 Olympic Games. They put their sport well and truly on the map for Australian fans.

Prior to Burns' gold and Trenton's silver, taekwondo was largely dismissed by Australians as just another form of Asian martial arts.

The eight-member team did not even have a press conference to announce their arrival at the Olympic village and when the squad was announced in August, just two media representatives bothered to show up.

But, particularly after Burns' stunning win on the opening night of competition, that has all changed.

Suddenly everyone wanted a piece of this unheralded gold medal-winner, who happened to be the daughter of '60s pop icon, Ronnie Burns. Just as importantly, people wanted to know more about her sport.

After such a highpoint, the momentum faltered slightly on days two and three, with no Australian qualifying for a final, but Trenton picked it up again by winning silver in the men's over 80kg class on the final day.

Their efforts placed Australia second behind Korea, which finished with four medals. It was a tremendous honor given Korea is the home of taekwondo and Australia has never before been considered strong in the sport.

Clearly, this is about to change.

"For the last few years Australia has performed well internationally, but we just haven't got the exposure," the 23-year-old Trenton said.

"Now we've proved we can be successful in this sport. The rest of the world are keeping in touch with Korea and maybe one day we'll catch up with them."

Trenton thrilled the big crowds at the State Sports Centre with his aggressive approach, despite the fact he gave a height and weight advantage to his opposition. His brave run came to an end at the hands of Korean giant Kim Kyong-Hun, who towered 16cm taller than the 180cm Trenton.

He had never fought Kim before and it showed. Trenton admitted it was back to the

drawing board if it meant making it to No.1 in the world.

Burns, meanwhile, will reap the rewards of her gold medal — the first for taekwondo — that caught all Australian sports fans by surprise.

Her website, which pushes her passion for the sport, will now be tapped into by a new legion of fans. Sponsors will come knocking, keen to be associated with this articulate woman who has scaled the heights of a foreign sport.

Burns' win, in front of her celebrity father Ronnie, was all guts.

The 26-year-old endured two painful kicks to the groin and a frustrating five-minute delay because of a faulty scoreboard, but she still had too much for Cuba's Urbia Melendez Rodriguez.

Burns hoped her win would help lift the sport in Australia.

"It's fast, it's powerful, it's dynamic ... I really hope people see that and get involved," she said.

The Australian successes aside, taekwondo's official debut at the Olympic Games (it was a demonstration sport in Seoul in 1988) was marred by adjudicating controversies.

There were howls of discontent from France and Hungary, while Denmark's coach staged an on-court protest, claiming the Australian players were being unfairly favored in front of their home fans.

But there were also some moving stories. Cuba's male under 80kg fighter Angel

Valodia Matos Fuentes dedicated his gold medal to his mother, who died after he had left for Sydney.

In the middle of her campaign, Australian women's over 67kg player Tanya White learned her father had suffered a stroke. After visiting him in hospital, she arrived back at the stadium just in time for her match but, understandably, was in no condition to win.

Taekwondo also produced Vietnam's first Olympic medallist.

Tran Hieu Ngan celebrated like she was the winner — not the loser — of her final in the women's under 57kg against Korea's Jung Jae-Eun. It was later revealed her silver medal had broken Vietnam's drought at the Games.

Left: Daniel Trenton found the towering 196cm Korean, Kim Hyong-Hun, too big to overpower.

Top: More Korean joy as Sun Hee Lee celebrates winning the 67kg class.

Above: Cuba was another of the strong nations in the taekwondo tournament, with Manuel Estrada Garibay winning the 80kg division.

Opposite page: Number One. Australia's Lauren Burns knows she has won gold.

HOCKEY

Australia's Hockeyroos were dubbed the greatest team the nation has seen after winning back-to-back golds in women's hockey. It was a fitting finale to international competition for triple Olympic gold medallist Rechelle Hawkes and the team's mentor, Ric Charlesworth.

Above: Piet-Hein Geeris and Dutch captain Stephan Veen celebrate back-to-back Olympic gold.

Opposite page: They would pose for photographs all night. The Hockeyroos show off their spoils.

Opening spread: In a spray of water, Hockeyroo Jenny Morris thumps another ball towards goal.

History was against them both. No hockey team, neither men's nor women's, had successfully defended an Olympic crown since India strung together six in a row from 1932-1956.

Still, Australia's golden Hockeyroos and the Netherlands Orangemen started favorites and, at the end, their national anthems that had been pumped out over the reconfigured football grounds of Morris Brown College in Atlanta four years earlier, echoed across the waters to Sydney. But the way the Olympic hockey tournament unfolded to its predictable conclusion for the gold medals was not so conventional.

It was crazy, almost everyone would conclude. Grand teams, such as the Dutch women, who have 300 artificial pitches to train on at home, were beaten by the Chinese. China, the last team of 10 to qualify for the Games had just 300 players, spread over six clubs, from which to choose. "It's the Olympic Games", frustrated coaches would say to explain how the in-built pressure of the event — rather than that of the opponents — influenced inexplicable results.

It was Russian Roulette. The gun team was the Hockeyroos, Australia's Dream Team of superbly-prepared women who were undefeated and virtually unchallenged over eight matches. They extended their unbeaten sequence at the Olympic Games to a record 18 and became the first women's hockey team to win consecutive gold since the sport was added to the Games program in 1980. There could have been no more appropriate send-off for their svengali Dr Richard Charlesworth or their captain Rechelle Hawkes, who became just the third Australian — behind Dawn Fraser and Andrew Hoy — to win gold three times in the same event.

The team that kept dodging bullets was the Netherlands men, who like the Hockeyroos, remained world and Olympic champions — but without the conviction of the Australian women. The Dutch walked off the State Hockey Centre field, a venue in desperate need of a snappier name, after losing 2-0 to Pakistan in their final Pool A match thinking they had missed the semi-finals.

Their coach Maurits Hendriks noted his men, "having been on top of the mountain for so

long, winning everything", had subconsciously been so scared of falling off that their fear ultimately became reality.

Two hours later, they had a most unlikely reprieve — Great Britain beat Germany 2-1, tipping the Germans out of the semi-finals and ushering back the Dutch. As the hooter sounded, the Brits, who needed the win to keep a critical top-six finish in their grasp, looked to the heavens as they opened with rain. It was the miracle that washed away Dutch tears that would be replaced by others, in particular those of Kookaburra centre-half Brent Livermore.

The Netherlands did not win another game in regulation, but kept gold by beating Australia's Kookaburras and Korea 5-4 in penalty shoot-outs in the semi-final and final respectively.

Amazingly, the best players for the Kookaburras — Livermore — and Korea — striker and player of the tournament Seung-Tae Song — missed flicks, both to the left post, in the penalty shoot-outs.

Just as Hawkes had her dream farewell, so did Dutch captain Stephan Veen, who not only scored a hat-trick in the 3-3 draw during the regulation 70 minutes of the final, but also the winning penalty in the shoot-out. Australia was the only nation to go through both the men's and women's hockey tournaments with their teams not losing a match in regulation. But the dream of a golden double for the Kookaburras and Hockeyroos became nothing more than a fantasy for the fans and continued frustration for the Kookaburras, unquestionably the unluckiest team in Olympic history.

They played 505 minutes of hockey, won four matches, drew three, scored a tournament-high 18 goals, conceded a tournament-low nine ... and won bronze by beating Pakistan 6-3.

The gold medallist Dutch, by comparison, won just two matches. No night was crazier than the second Tuesday of the pool matches when the Dutch had their great escape.

On that stormy night, India had one foot in a semi-final until Poland scored an equaliser to force a 1-1 draw with 90 seconds to play.

Like Australia, Pakistan had reached the semi-finals unbeaten but were tactically outsmarted by the Koreans in the play-off. Like the Netherlands, Korea reached the final on a miracle.

The recurring nightmare of the Kookaburras going without gold goes on.

The lingering image from this Games will

be Livermore, collapsing to his knees in tears after his flick was nicked by the stick of Dutch goalkeeper Ronald Jansen.

It is a moment that will consign Livermore to eternal recall on trival pursuit quiz nights.

It is a harsh way to claim immortality for such a talented and decent player who, through his midfield play, had given the Kookaburras their best chance to win their first Olympic gold medal.

There were tears of different kinds in the women's series with a very different format to the men's competition and one that ultimately rewarded teams that played to win.

Argentina, the Lions, advanced from Pool A, but did not get to keep any of its points from the preliminary rounds after the teams were re-ranked for the Super Six.

The top-three teams from each pool were only allowed to carry forward points from matches against their Super Six colleagues and Argentina lost both its matches to Pool A rivals Australia and Spain.

The Argentineans cried when faced with the imposing task of winning all three games against Pool B qualifers to make the final. They cried after completing the miracle with a 7-1 rout of New Zealand.

They cried on winning silver to an Australian team they acknowledged as the greatest of all time.

By comparison the Hockeyroos advanced to the final with ease, dropping just one point with a 1-1 draw against Spain.

Charlesworth's public pronouncments were few, but his final words after the 3-1 win against Argentina in the final, that closed his eight-year reign over 253 matches with 198 wins, 25 draws and just 30 losses, were: ''I am proud of you.''

So was Australia — and the sport of women's hockey that has been advanced by the Hockeyroos' refusal to accept limits to their brilliance.

Above: History was against the Dutch repeating its Atlanta triumph, but they held their nerve throughout the tournament.

Left: The Kookaburras say thank you and goodbye to the partisan Australian crowd after winning bronze.

Opposite: Party time. Australia's James Elmer jumps on Craig Victory.

Above: Nikki Hudson pushes forward for Australia in the gold medal game against Argentina.

Right: Jenny Morris (left) tackles Argentine Ayelen Stepnik, with Kate Starre looking on.

Opposite page, top: A well-deserved lap of honor for the dominant Hockeyroos.

Opposite page, below left to right: Rechelle Hawkes, the only surviving member of Australia's 1988 Seoul Olympic winning team, celebrates an early goal. On the siren the Australian co-captain was mobbed by teammates and received one of the loudest cheers when she accepted her third gold medal.

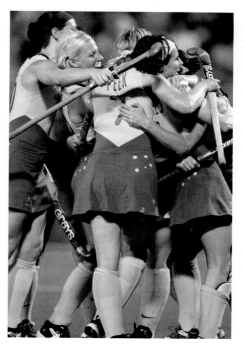

Above: A heart-rending moment for Brett Livermore. The Dutch team celebrates its passage into the gold medal game after Livermore missed a sudden-death penalty stroke.

Right: The Netherlands' Marten Eikelboom looks entirely comfortable with his team's performance.

Above and left: Crowds at the State Hockey Centre, no matter whose colors they wore, were extremely vocal. The hockey tournament attracted sell-out crowds throughout.

Right: Adam Commens enjoys a goal against Spain.
Below left: Australian goalie Damon Diletti shows a clean pair of heels.
Below right: Jay Stacy was always busy looking for opportunities up forward.

Opposite page, top: Striker James Elmer puts Australia into attack.
Opposite page, bottom left: Another Kookaburra forward, Troy Elmer puts the pressure on.
Opposite page, bottom right: Michael Brennan fends off Spain's Xavier Ribas.

Left: German Britta Becker tangled with Great Britain's Mandy Nicholson.

Below left: Briton Kate Walsh argued with the umpire as Australia celebrated a controversial victory. Australian claimed the British had breached the rules twice and the match should end. Australia's Alyson Annan pointed out British goalkeeper Hilary Rose was on the field without a helmet and, secondly, the British team had not stopped the penalty corner outside the circle before they took their strike at goal, as demanded by hockey's rules.

Below right: Argentinian joy, Augustina Garcia is hugged by Karina Masotta after the goal that sunk Spain's gold medal hopes.

Opposite, top: Julie Towers gave it her all pushing in a penalty corner against Argentina in the preliminary rounds.

Opposite, below left: Katrina Powell asks the umpire whether that shot was her second free hit.

Opposite, below right: Nikki Hudson crashes over the top of Great Britain's Pauline Scott.

GYMNASTICS

GYMNASTICS

The power, the grace, the controversy. Gymnastics had it all in Sydney with the hottest of favorites finding the competition too hot to handle. Australia celebrated its first gymnastics medal in the new discipline of trampoline, but hopes of wider success for the host nation faded early.

Above: Russian dynamo Alexei Nemov carried the expectation of a country on his back, and came through brilliantly.

Opposite page: Nemov, on the pommel horse, was largely responsible for Russia taking bronze in the team events.

Opening spread: Alina Kabaeva of Russia was the hottest of hot favorites in rhythmic gymnastics, but claimed only bronze.

No fewer than 18 gold medals were awarded in gymnastics but the one that was taken from tiny Andreea Raducan of Romania will be remembered throughout Olympic history.

Raducan was clearly the best all-around gymnast at the competition. As a 16-year-old, she won the right to be called the world's best gymnast. But by the time she turned 17 a few days later she had been stripped of gold because she had taken a cold medicine containing pseudo-ephedrine prescribed by the team doctor. The gold medal was awarded to her team mate Simona Amanar but no one, least of all Amanar, really believed justice was done.

The International Olympic Committee enforced the strict letter of the law. Francois Carrard, director-general of the IOC, frankly admitted the medicine gave Raducan no competitive advantage whatsoever but said a zero tolerance drug policy gave the IOC no choice but to take the gold medal away. Raducan was allowed to keep the team gold she helped Romania win and also the silver won on the vault. Both further testimony to her dominace of the women's competition at the SuperDome.

In individual apparatus, Russian Elena Zamolodtchikova won two gold medals, outshining her more famous but equally glamorous team mate, Svetlana Khorkina. When Khorkina withdrew from the vault competition, her place was taken by Zamolodtchikova who went on to win. One day later, with Khorkina leading on the floor exercise would Zamolodtchikova return the favor and play Khorkina into the gold medal? Not likely. With a superb performance of grace and athleticism, Zamolodtchikova swept past Khorkina to grab her second gold. Khorkina, a stunningly theatrical gymnast, was the central character in an embarassing bungle by officials when the vault for the women's apparatus final was set 5cm too low for the first two rotations of the women's final. She crashed at her first vault, costing her any chance of a medal, and although she, along with the others who had competed at the wrong height, was offered another chance she declined, ostensibly to ensure fitness for other finals the following day. Ultimately, she did win gold — on her favorite apparatus, the uneven bars.

While Khorkina did not quite live up to expectations, countryman Alexei Nemov more than made up for any failings. Nemov carried the Russian team on his back to grab the bronze medal in the team event. Then, in a heroic performance over a week of competition,

also picked up the individual all around gold medal. That was followed by silver on the floor, bronze on the pommel horse and parallel bars and then finally gold on the horizontal bar. A total of two gold, one silver and three bronze made him the star of artistic gymnastics in Sydney and established him as a legend back home in Russia where his baby boy he had never seen awaited his return. Nemov was also the consummate showman — always smiling, laughing and giving generously of himself to his fellow competitors and the crowds. In a sport that can tend to take itself a bit too seriously, Nemov was a popular champion.

The Australian campaign started disastrously and did not get much better. On Australia's first apparatus, the vault, one of its most accomplished gymnasts, Allana Slater, crashed twice. With that, the team had its back to the wall. Hopes of a team bronze medal looked slim. Despite a revival on the other apparatus, Australia finished seventh — just a few points outside the teams final. Slater and Trudy McIntosh who had also set their sights on appearing in apparatus finals were also disappointed. But Lisa Skinner, whose exotic Arab Princess routine charmed the judges and drew world-wide attention to her talents, made the final of the floor exercise. Only a slip in that final spoiled her otherwise splendid Olympic experience.

However things did get better, through another Queenslander. Ji Wallace, who learned trampoline in his Brisbane backyard, won Australia's first gymnastics medal, taking silver behind the master of the sport, Alexandre Moskalenko of Russia.

This was a exceptional Olympic campaign by Wallace, whose mother forced him to take up the sport because of her fears that, unsupervised in his backyard, he might hurt himself.

The gymnastics events finished, fittingly, with high drama in the rhythmic routines. After Russia won the group event, another Russian Alina Kabaeva was a hot favorite to win the individual gold medal. But a slip on the hoop routine, meant one of the odds-on Games favorites could win only bronze behind her team mate, Yulia Barsukova.

All in all, gymnastics, a sport of such grace and beauty, had its fair share of drama in Sydney.

Above: Brazil's hoop and ribbon team were crowd pleasers.

Right: Japan also performed strongly in the teams event.

Opposite page, top left: Yulia Barsukova of Russia jumps through hoops on her way to gold.

Opposite page, top right: Incredible flexibility shown by Spain's Almudena Cid with the ball.

Opposite page, bottom left: Australia's leading rhythmic gymnast Dani LeRay was spectacular in her rope routine.

Opposite page, bottom right: All-around gold for Yulia Barsukova.

Right: Russia's Alina Kabaeva enjoyed her moment in the spotlight during the gymnastics gala, before things turned sour for her in the all-around final, where she finished third.

Opposite page: Teams events featured crowd-pleasing routines, especially the Japanese (top) and the Greek team (bottom). The Greeks, performing with the clubs, won a bronze medal.

Above: Australia's Ji Wallace went into the Olympic Games ranked fifth in the world but pulled out a blinding performance, claiming silver in the trampoline.

Above right: Oxana Tsyhuleva of Russia looks headed for disaster, competing to win silver in trampoline, a discipline which made its Olympic debut.

Opposite page: The power to perform. Ivan Ivankov of Bulgaria prepares for one of the most demanding of the men's apparatus, the rings.

Above: Russian diva Svetlana Khorkina's hands are coated in the resin used to avoid slippage on the floor, vault and uneven bar routines. Khorkina, though, suffered serious misses on the uneven bars to derail her campaign for gold.

Opposite page, top: The grace and beauty of gymnastics in the uneven bar routine by China's Xuan Liu.

Opposite, below far left: Khorkina in a spinning dismount from the beam.

Opposite, below middle: Australian team member Brooke Walker defies gravity on the beam. Australia finished in seventh place, fractionally out of the team's final.

Opposite, below right: Ekaterina Lobazniouk of Russia wows the crowd during the floor exercise.

Left: All around gold medallist, Andreea Raducan of Romania celebrates like a gymnast should – standing on the shoulders of her coach, Octavian Bellu.

Top: But her joy was short-lived. Raducan tested positive for pseudo-ephedrine after taking cold medicine and was stripped of her gold medal. With Romanian Olympic Committee head Ion Tiriac, she headed for the appeals court.

Above: Australia's Lisa Skinner had the host nation's best finish ever in the all-around final, with ninth, after being in the bronze medal position going into the final rotation.

Opposite page, top: A picture of sheer strength. Tsukahara Naoya, of Japan on the rings.

Opposite, bottom left: Aowei Xing demonstrated supreme control on the floor, helping China to the team gold medal.

Opposite, bottom middle: All around gold-medallist Alexei Nemov of Russia, pictured on the parallel bars, dominated the men's event.

Opposite, bottom right Spain's gold medal winning vaulter Gervasion Deffer.

VOLLEYBALL

Stage fright. It took a while for Natalie Cook and Kerri Pottharst to get used to the crowd being on their side for a change. There was a party every day in the makeshift stands at Bondi Beach, celebrating Australia's first medal in the sport, while indoors, the national teams were far from disgraced.

Above: Cuba is jubilant after winning the indoor volleyball women's gold, over Brazil.

Opposite page: Kiss the sand – beach volleyball gold medallists Natalie Cook and Kerri Pottharst get down to give thanks on Bondi Beach.

Opening spread: Just the two of us. Natalie Cook and Kerri Pottharst proved to be Australia's most formidable duo.

Plagued by controversy and howls of protests in the lead up to the Olympic Games, Bondi's beach volleyball stadium turned out to be one of the success stories of Sydney. Unwanted by locals, the impressive 10,000-seat stadium turned out to be the Games' unofficial party venue, generating an electric atmosphere fuelled by a dancing, Mexican-waving crowd and loud music throughout the entire tournament.

It was something Australia's greatest hopes Natalie Cook and Kerri Pottharst initially had trouble coming to terms with, but by the time their first serve rocketed over the net it felt good to be on home sand. Cook and Pottharst were the superstars of the tournament, clinching victory in an unbelievable final against Brazilian champions Shelda Bede and Adriana Behar.

The Australians literally walked across hot coals on their way to Olympic glory, splitting up after their bronze medal in Atlanta after a personality clash before realising, 18 months later, that their best chance of a gold medal lay with each other. To help themselves mentally prepare, they took up fire-walking and walking across broken glass to reinforce the idea that nothing was impossible. Then, to refine their physical performance, Cook and Pottharst often trained against male competitors, hoping to take their game to the next level for the competition at Bondi.

Their win was something of an upset, considering they beat the most successful women's partnership in beach volleyball history in Bede and Behar. But to the crowd, it was certainly not unexpected, backing them to the hilt with rabid support.

The lucrative international circuit sees Australian players away most of the year. This was the first time they had played in a major event without a hostile crowd. All Australian pairings admitted to suffering "stage fright", opening the tournament with mixed results.

Cook and Pottharst won, as did Tania Gooley and Pauline Manser, but not all of the Australian contingent were lucky enough to escape with a warning. Annette Huygens Tholen and Sarah Straton were just pipped by third-ranked Americans Jenny Jordan Johnson and Annett Davis in their first round clash, while in the men's, Matt Grinlaubs and Josh Slack were no match for Brazilians Emanuel Rego and Jose Loiola.

But the biggest blow was suffered by Australia's top-seeded men's pair of Julien Prosser and Lee Zahner, who lost their battle with nerves to last-seeded Mexicans Juan Ibarra and Joel Sotelo.

Cook and Pottharst turned to Olympic legends Dawn Fraser and Herb Elliott and fellow Olympians Pat Rafter and Rennae Stubbs for help in dealing with the pressures of home-town support, and it started to pay dividends as they were the only Australians left standing by the semi-finals. They looked to be settling into their rhythm by disposing of fifth-seeded Brazilians Sandra Pires and Adriana Samuel 15-6 in the semi-final to win through to the gold-medal showdown.

In front of a rocking capacity crowd in the final, the Australians started the first set confidently, were quickly chased down by the Brazilians, and then found themselves a in deep trouble when they trailed 6-10. But playing with a motto to simply enjoy themselves, the Australians roared back to draw level 11-all. Cook, almost unbelievably, sent down an ace to win the set, and deliver a body blow to the confidence of the Brazilians, from which they did not recover.

The "ace" was a serve towards Bede that struck the net and hesitated for a second before dropping pathetically on to the sand on the Brazilians' side of the net.

To the Australians — on the court and in the stands — it was the sweetest sight of all.

It was a disappointing competition for the Brazilians, with their men's team of Ze Marco Melo and Ricardo Santos losing the gold-medal play-off to unheralded Americans Dain Blanton and Eric Fonoimoana, a team that would not have even qualified for the Games had injury not cut into the US squad.

At the indoor volleyball, Australia's men and women had no medals to their names, but still enjoyed a successful tournament at their Olympic debut.

Qualifying through the home-nation rule and going into the tournament as massive underdogs with world rankings of 16 (men) and 27 (women), the Australians proved to be surprise packets with their tenacious play. That saw the men's team achieve the remarkable feat of winning through to the quarter finals, and then showing it was not over-awed by the occasion, taking a set off the world-champion Italian team. The women had no such luck in making a final, but they did register a four-set win over Kenya, sparking scenes of unbridled jubilation among the rookie team. As expected though, it was the world volleyball heavyweights that won the day in Sydney, with the Cuban women grabbing a third gold while Yugoslavia was crowned men's champion.

Above: Fighting for gold. Natalie Cook spikes one past Adriana Behar of Brazil.

Left: Danja Musch of Germany was a picture of balance and concentration.

Far left: France's Cecile Rigaux celebrates a point against Germany.

Opposite page, top: Party central. The Beach Volleyball stadium at Bondi was a hit venue.

Opposite, below left: Love in the sand – Dain Blanton and and Eric Fonoimoana of the USA were excited to win the men's gold.

Opposite, below right: Australia's Julien Prosser keeps the ball alive. He and Lee Zahner were considered medal hopes but were bundled out in the fourth round.

Above: The cost to the fingers of elite volleyball.

Far left: Regia Torres of Cuba slams the ball home for another winner.

Left: Australia's women were unfancied in the tournament, but impressed with their tenacious play. Priscilla Ruddle goes for the spike against Brazil.

Opposite page, top: Andrija Geric tries to keep the ball alive for Yugoslavia, from Russia's Rouslan Olikhver and Roman Iakovlev.

Opposite page, bottom left: Ivan Miljkovic of Yugoslavia spikes the ball while Russian Roman Iakovlev and Alexei Kazakov defend. Yugoslavia won the gold in three sets.

Opposite page, bottom right: Cuban Regia Bell showed her relief after winning the gold medal against Russia.

WORDS | PETER JENKINS

CANOE/KAYAK

Penrith did not provide a fertile environment for Australian gold but, until the last day of the canoe/kayak regatta, it had been a paddler's paradise.

That all changed when gale force winds roared through the course, churning previously placid waters.

Above: After boxing kangaroos and Fatso the Wombat, kayaker Andrew Trim chose an emu mascot when he won silver with Daniel Collins.

Opposite page: The best Australia could do was silver, to Trim and Collins in the men's K2 500m.

Better late than never. Long after they should have been preparing to attend closing ceremony celebrations, Australians Andrew Trim and Daniel Collins were standing on the dais at Penrith Lakes having silver medals hung around their necks.

The last day of canoe-kayak competition, after five mornings of perfect conditions, held a horrid surprise for the paddling fraternity.

Gale-force winds lashed the course, reaching speeds of 60kmh. Whitecaps and waves replaced what had been, for almost a week, a smooth as glass regatta surface.

After a six-hour delay — punctuated by the possibility of staging the finals the day after the Olympic flame had been extinguished or even cancelling the last six races and not awarding medals — relieved officials were eventually able to confirm a start.

And when they did, Australia added two medals to their overall tally for the Games.

Trim and Collins, hoping for gold, settled for silver in the men's K2 500m. They followed the bronze medal performance of three-time Olympian, Australia's Katrin Borchert in the women's K1 500m.

It was almost 5pm before the men's crew stepped up on to the podium, with the late finish ending plans to trek to Sydney Olympic Park with their young families in tow to attend the finale.

But the metal made up for their cancelled journey. Besides, the drama of the day was adventure enough.

The man-made flatwater and whitewater courses in Sydney's west had given up no gold for Australian rowers, nor any to the canoe-kayak contingent, when Trim, 31, and Collins, 29, made their dash for glory.

European crews dominated both regattas and they did so again in the event the Brisbane pair — bronze medallists from Atlanta in 1996 — had targeted in their third and final Olympic Games together.

Hungarians Zoltan Kammerer and Botond Storcz completed an all the way win in 1:47.05 to edge out the Australians (1:47.89) with Germany's Ronald Rauhe and Tim Weiskoetter almost one second adrift in third.

Borchert, 31, headed into the day with dual medal hopes. She realised her goal with a bronze in the women's K1 500m, behind Italy's Josefa Idem Guerrini and Canada's world champion Caroline Brunet. But in the women's K2 500m final, there was no fairytale finish for Borchert and Anna Wood. They finished sixth with Germany, Hungary and Poland grabbing the top three places. Borchert, who represented Germany at her first Games in 1992, has declared Athens is on her agenda but Wood has announced her retirement.

The two-medal finish for the Australians followed disappointing early rounds. Barcelona gold medallist Clint Robinson, who also took bronze in Atlanta, did not advance past the semi finals of the men's K1000m. The women's K4 500m, the men's K2 1000m and men's K4 1000m also missed reaching medal races. Nathan Baggaley in the men's K1 500m was another to dip out in the semi finals, his

omission from the finals laced with controversy. There were newspaper reports in Bulgaria claiming their star paddler Petar Merkov had tested positive to a banned substance two months before the Games.

The allegations were not confirmed, he finished ahead of Baggaley in the semi finals and went on to claim silver behind Norway's Knut Holman. Merkov also took silver behind Holman in the men's K1 1000m.

While Holman was a standout in the men's divisions, German supermum Birgit Fischer took two gold medals.

Fischer was elevated to the pantheon of Olympic greats with seven gold in a glittering career going back to 1980. Her career could have been even more breathtaking but for the East German boycott of the 1984 Games in Los Angeles.

The 38-year-old mother of two won gold in Moscow in 1980, two gold and a silver at Seoul, gold and silver in Barcelona, gold and silver in Atlanta and two gold in Sydney.

After 20 years as a leader in the sport, Fischer has announced her retirement.

In whitewater events, where capacity crowds were thrilled by the canoe and kayak slalom; Australians Robin Bell in the men's C1 and Danielle Woodward in the women's K1 had their eyes on a podium finish. Woodward qualified 14th after her two runs in qualifying. In the final, her first run brought four penalties and a 10th ranking. Her second run was clear, sixth best in the field, for an overall placing of eighth.

The gold medal went to Stepanka Hilgertova of the Czech Republic.

Slovakian Michal Martikan, a former teenage prodigy, was the gold medal favorite in the men's C1. He qualified at the head of the field for the final but lost out in the end to Frenchman Tony Estanguet. Martikan finished with silver. As for Bell, he finished the two qualifying runs in fifth position and in the final, but a 10th in his last run gave him an overall finish of ninth.

Above: Welcome to the washing machine.
Austrlaia's Katrin Borchert battled winds and
waves on her way to bronze in the women's
K1 500m

Above left: Queen of kayaks. A seventh gold medal to Germany's Birgit Fischer in the women's K4 500m.

Top: No such joy for Australia's women four.

Above: The men's K4 also failed to make the final.

Left: To the winners, the cheers. C2 500m gold medallists Ferenc Novak and Imre Pula of Hungary.

Above: Mitica Pricop and Florin Popescu on their way to glory in the C2 1000m.

Right: The Italians created some unnecessary drag, but it was after Antonio Rossi and Beniamino Bonomi claimed gold in the K2 1000m.

Above: Not an easy day out for Irena Pavelkova of the Czech Republic in the K1.

Far left: France's Tony Estanguet on his way to Olympic gold in the C1.

Left: Australian veteran Danielle Woodward pulled out the run of her lfie to place a creditable eighth overall in her final Olympic appearance.

Top: Almost swamped by whitewater, Frank Addison and Wilfred Forgues of France contest the C2. After gold in Atlanta, they failed to place on the podium in Sydney.

Middle: Straining to gain every second, Swiss paddler Sandra Friedli on her way to ninth in the women's K1.

Bottom: Kai Swoboda and Andrew Farrance dig in during the men's C2.

Opposite: Australia's Robin Bell threatened the leaders throughout the C1, before finishing ninth in his first Olympic Games appearance.

WATER POLO

WATER POLO

A bolt from the blue — an appropriate enough description for Yvette Higgins' mesmerising last-second goal that gave Australia gold as women's water polo made its Olympic debut. For a team that was largely responsible for the women's inclusion, it was a just reward.

Top: Australian coach Istvan Gorgenyi celebrates gold with Taryn Woods.

Above: The Hungarian team takes to the water after defeating Russia for gold in the men's event.

Opposite page: The Australian women's team thanks its supporters after defeating the USA.

Opening spread: The formidable sight of Liz Weekes in Australia's goal.

The clock on the wall showed just 1.3 more seconds. Yvette Higgins' left hand held a ball, a century of sexual inequality and a lifetime of personal sacrifice.

Too often, time is the master of humanity but on this occasion it proved no match for what Higgins had to offer.

Within a second, the ball was in the net and a world record water polo crowd of 17,000 erupted to celebrate Australia's astonishing 4-3 victory over the United States, in the first-ever women's Olympic water polo final.

Eight days later, and 44 years after the most infamous match in the sport's history, Hungary eclipsed Russia 13-6 to mark the centenary of the men's sport in the Games with an emphatic victory.

In this case, time did prevail, diluting the bloody spite of the 1956 clash at the Melbourne Olympic Games between Hungary and the Soviet Union.

In its place was a passion of far greater nobility etched on the faces of the winners and emphasised further by the despair of the vanquished.

But Olympic gold will only continue to be the ultimate prize, if the journey is trod by combatants who are worthy.

The hulking, volatile, aggressive men's teams from Yugoslavia and Croatia proved they were.

Given the tense political situation between the two countries, officials feared there might have been spectator unrest during a crucial group match at Ryde between the two unbeaten teams.

Police quelled a mini-riot in the stands when the teams played in Perth at the 1998 world championships and sadly, before this Olympic match, players had received threats and so asked their families not to attend.

When raw emotion is such an integral part of sport it becomes an unfair burden on the players, yet they subdued their acknowledgement of the crowd before the match, reduced their celebration after each goal and accepted every referee's decision without question.

Late in the game with scores level, Croatian coach Neven Kovacevic instinctively leapt to his feet, shouting instructions — only to be restrained by one of his players.

If the 4-all draw was a triumph for diplomacy, there was a touch of magic about the Australian women's gold medal which came after a week notable for its ripped costumes.

This was poetic justice. One hundred years after men began playing the sport in the Olympic Games, this was the team that marched on a Sydney meeting of the aquatics international governing body, FINA to — successfully — press for the inclusion of women.

In front of raucous, parochial crowds, the Australians lost just one match on their path to start firm favorites in their

semi-final match with Russia but trailed 6-4 inside the last five minutes.

Coach Istvan Gorgenyi later said he doubted he had "another rabbit" to pull from his hat before veteran Debbie Watson grabbed one back and vice-captain Naomi Castle equalised with 90 seconds remaining.

Backed by magnificent defence, skipper Bridgette Gusterson scored the winner 43 seconds from the finish to earn a gold medal berth against the US, the most improved team in the world this year and conqueror of the No1 ranked Dutch, 6-5, in the other semi.

In the final, Liz Weekes, in goal, and Bronwyn Mayer were standouts for Australia but defence ruled and, with less than two minutes remaining, it was 2-all.

Considering the low scores, a late, long

bomb from Castle appeared a match-winner but amazingly two more goals were scored in the last 13 seconds.

Brenda Villa levelled for the US before Australia surged and Higgins was fouled outside seven metres. Because of her distance from goal, her direct shot was legal but caused great confusion.

American journalists, foiled in their hopes of writing about an unexpected gold from a quaint sport, instead became enthused about re-telling a tale of being scuttled Down Under.

But to the anguish of the reporters, US coach Guy Baker and his players were gracious amid defeat and despair, leaving the writers nowhere to go for the necessary color.

After the women's success, expectations for the Australian men's

team were, perhaps, unfairly heightened. The Sharks finished eighth, which was a fair representation of their talent.

Australia won just one of its eight matches and drew two.

Not all the Sharks appeared comfortable to compete at this level, some lacking variety and flair in attack.

Daniel Marsden, Andrei Kovalenko, Sean Boyd and Eddie Denis were consistently solid.

Spain was without star centre-forward Ivan Perez, who did not receive a clearance from his native Cuba.

But the Spaniards almost pulled off a farewell miracle for skipper Manuel Estiarte, competing in his sixth consecutive Olympic Games.

Estiarte's speed and deft touch lifted Spain to the semis where it lost 8-7 to Russia, but only after 16 minutes of extra-time and sudden death.

In the other high-quality semi, Hungary importantly kept Yugoslav ace Aleksandar Sapic, the tournament's top scorer, to one goal and won 8-7.

After 20 years in the Olympic wilderness, Hungary won its seventh Games gold in a complete display, combining great goal-keeping, individual brilliance and an unstoppable variety and structure on extra-man plays.

Above left: Australia's Debbie Watson lets rip in a torn costume during the semi-final against Russia.

Left: The Australian team enjoyed strong victories throughout the tournament.

Opposite, top: Reflections of brilliance. The Hungarian team prepares to enter the water.

Opposite, bottom left: Peter Biros of Hungary signifies his country's return to No.1 in water polo.

Opposite, bottom right: Australia's Eddie Dennis was in goal for Australia against Yugoslavia.

WRESTLING

Australia recorded just two wins for the wrestling tournament, but the story of the Olympic Games belonged to the Nigerian-born Canadian wrestler, Daniel Igali. Having lost his adopted mother last year, his inspiration for gold came from a dream.

Above: A test to make sure his gold medal was the genuine article, Canada's Daniel Igali scored an emotion-packed victory.

Opposite: Fingertips keep Germany's Othmar Kuhner off the mat in his 58kg bout against Arif Abdullayev of Azerbaijan.

The image was singular. Wrestling's greatest ever performer, Alexandre Kareline, stopped competing with four seconds left in overtime.

A look of surprise gripped the great Russian's features as he stared at the first man to conquer him in 13 years of international competition — American Rulon Gardner, a country boy from Wyoming.

Kareline, the 130kg Greco-Roman icon, the likes of whom are never likely to be seen again, was shooting for a fourth straight Olympic gold in the one event.

Victory would have completed what has been a remarkable career, including nine world championships and 13 other European championships, but a new king was crowned.

So highly was Gardner's achievement regarded, he was asked to carry the American flag in the closing ceremony.

The Sydney 2000 Olympic Games will be best remembered as the end of a reign with Kareline likely to retire, leaving the sport in Russia to his heir apparent, Adam Saitev.

Saitev has lived in Kareline's shadow for many years despite his dominance in the under 76kg freestyle division and, at this Games, the under 85kg division, but this could be his greatest opportunity.

In his rise for gold during these Games, Saitev locked wills with Australia's leading wrestler, Igor Praporshchikov, and, while pushed throughout by the Australian, Saitev's immense ability ensured that he failed to concede a point.

The quietly-spoken Russian only conceded a handful of points in his drive for Olympic success, eventually powering past Cuba's 1999 world champion Yoel Romero for the ultimate prize.

Praporshchikov, like all of the Australians, competed with distinction without always tasting success.

That was left to Gabriel Szerda — national under 97kg champion — who posted the first of only two Australian wins when downing Canada's Dean Schmeichel 4-2.

So eager were the home crowd that Szerda was cheered through every point and lifted to parry every attack.

When victory was assured, the Sydney Exhibition Centre was gripped with screams of euphoria. The second success fell to Cameron Johnston, the under 69kg freestyle representative, who won by forfeit over Ruslan Veliyev of Kazakhstan.

One wrestler who was unable to fulfil his dream of competing was Australia's Mushtaq Abdullah.

The giant wrestler was robbed of a second Olympic Games when a serious illness saw him shed 15kg in the week prior to his 130kg freestyle competition, leaving him bitterly disappointed. The Iraqi-born Australian had dedicated himself solely to performing at his optimum in Sydney, after being unable to wrestle in Atlanta because of citizenship restrictions.

One of the powers in freestyle wrestling was Iran. Supported by fanatical crowds, the Iranians continued to rise to the heights and finished with gold to pocket dynamo Alizero Dabir in the under 58kg division.

His success had the mainly Iranian crowd in fits of jubilation as flags were waved and painted faces roared.

But for emotion, nothing could equal the Olympic conquest of Nigerian-born Canadian Daniel Igali. The under 69kg champion had long planned to be in Sydney with his adopted mother Maureen Methney, only for cancer to steal her away from him just days after he had won the 1999 world championships.

Nevertheless, Igali said Methney was with him in his tenacious success, visiting him in a dream as he slept just hours before his gold medal bout and whispering, "I am proud of you."

Igali wept in remembrance atop the dais and his emotion was mirrored in the faces of those who knew of his journey.

As he walked around the hall he was saluted by a unified voice of encouragement and praised for his fortitude under immensely trying circumstances.

For Australia, it was a matter of counting the cost of a less-than impressive campaign and, immediately after the Games, it was announced there would be major changes in the sport

Top: In-Sub Kim (blue) of Korea gets the better of Kazakhstan's Yuriy Melnichenko.

Above: Australia's Ali Abdo (blue) found the going tough against Cuban Filiberto Ascuy in the 69kg division.

Left: Sweden's Mikael Ljungberg celebrates gold in the 97kg class.

Opposite page: The Sydney Exhibition Centre provided a world-class venue.

WORDS | NIKKI TUGWELL

HANDBALL

Scandinavia predictably dominated the handball tournament, with legions of rabid fans making the trip to Sydney. Australia, however, set about winning a new audience for an under-exposed sport and succeeded, playing in front of sell-out crowds.

Above: Handball is a national obsession in Norway with legions of fans travelling to Sydney just to attend their favorite sport.

Opposite, top left: Russia's Eduoard Kokcharov celebrates an upset win over Sweden to claim gold.

Opposite, top right: Denmark had been written off as "too old" to defend its Olympic crown. Here, Katrine Frueland sends down another lightning bolt in the game against Hungary.

Opposite, bottom: Australia's Taip Ramadani attacks against Spain.

The music to Mission Impossible formed an appropriate backdrop. Seemingly, the Australian men's handball team was being led into a minefield as it began its Olympic campaign against world champion, Sweden. There had been a major fear for the Australian team at the Olympic Games — that it would be embarrassed. Australia's handballers had failed to beat third and fourth division clubs in Europe and junior national teams. The men and women finished last at the 1999 world championships and neither had won a game.

The team, comprised mainly of expatriate Europeans, realised it needed to work as a unit and play a brand of handball that would endear Australian spectators to the sport.

So the players introduced two mandatory team rules. One, to speak English whenever they were together as a team and, two, to learn the Australian national anthem. After that, it was a matter of planting the seeds of self-belief and emulating the fight and spirit of the Anzacs.

It worked. The Australians won thousands of new supporters and handball became a buzz of the Olympic Games. Spectators, many seeing the sport for the first time, embraced it like a national pastime.

For many of the Australian players it was a thrill just to be on the same court as some of the superstars of the game, such as Magnus Wislander from Sweden and Talant Dujshebaev of Spain, Norway's Cecilia Leganger and Kjersti Grini or Camilla Anderson of Denmark. The Australians may have stolen the limelight but the Europeans remained the stars.

European, Asian and African crowds flocked to the handball games for a glimpse. Many fanatical Danish, Norwegian and Swedish fans travelled to Sydney just for the handball and bought tickets to every session. So when Australia faced Norway, the two could not come from more different worlds. Australian players struggle to buy handball shoes and equipment here, while the Norwegians have multi-million dollar endorsements from shoe companies.

Australia's top players are unknown here — the Norwegians are celebrities in their homeland, in the press every day and constantly in the public eye.

It was a highlight for Australia's women to compete with, let alone challenge, these stars. The scenes after the Australia-Norway match told the story. The siren sounded. The Australians, overcome with emotion, embraced each other, crying tears of joy.

Australia had just lost by 10 goals.

But they had thrown panic into the camp of the world champion and dominated Norway for 29 minutes and 40 seconds. It was a moment that will live with these Australian athletes forever.

Norway later featured in one of the upsets of the tournament — in the finals. Undefeated through the preliminary rounds, it was knocked out of gold-medal contention by Hungary in the semi-final and had to be content with bronze.

Denmark, which had finished sixth at the 1999 world championship, regained peak form to defend its Olympic crown in the women's event.

The other result that shocked the handball world was Sweden's loss to Russia in the gold-medal play-off, relegated to silver for the third consecutive Olympic Games. Spain came through for bronze.

For Australia, it knew it could not win many games, so the players set about winning the crowd.

Their theory: "If we win the crowd and win awareness for the sport in Australia, then we walk away winners."

They're still smiling.

WORDS | JEFF DUNNE

MODERN PENTATHLON

Under pressure to retain its place in the Olympic program, Sydney turned on a sight to gladden the hearts of modern pentathlon fans.

Sell-out crowds, gripping action and the debut of women all combined to make a winning formula.

Above: The first woman to win modern pentathlon gold, Britain's Stephanie Cook.

Opposite, top left: The best part of Australian Kitty Chiller's competition was the fencing.

Opposite, top right: No Russian stoicism for gold medallist Dmitry Svatkovsky.

Opposite, below right: Shooting, one of the five disciplines in modern pentathlon.

Baron Pierre de Coubertin would never have imagined it — the future of his pet sport captured in an image of two fair-skinned English girls wrapped in a Union Jack. The modern pentathlon in Sydney provided just such a picture and it was the success of women that should ensure a future for the five-discipline event.

The founder of the modern Games, de Coubertin was the driving force behind modern pentathlon's inclusion in the 1912 Games in Stockholm but it took until Sydney to admit women. The opportunity was not missed with Stephanie Cook, a 28-year-old doctor, providing one of the most dramatic finishes of the Games when she ran down the field to win the first gold medal for women in modern pentathlon.

Cook's journey had begun at 5am, sharing breakfast with pentathlon team-mate Kate Allenby and England's super heavyweight boxing hope Audley Harrison. By the end of the day, Cook and Allenby were celebrating with the Union Jack after winning gold and bronze while, across the Olympic city, Harrison had also won the gold medal bout in his division.

Despite backing in high places with Prince Albert of Monaco the honorary president of the world body, modern pentathlon will always be a sport battling for exposure and widespread appeal. It was under pressure to retain its position in the Olympic program but was saved after the decision to run the competition over one day rather than five. In Sydney, all the venues for the disciplines were within Sydney Olympic Park, resulting in the biggest crowds in the sport's history.

The riding section had the capacity crowd on the edge of their seats as the true test of the pentathletes was taking place — riding an unfamiliar horse around a show-jumping course of international standard. Many were thankful just to get through the ride in one piece, the European contestants in particular finding it difficult to control the robust Australian thoroughbreds. Three competitors were eliminated after dramatic falls.

After the ride, Cook was still well back in the field with American Emily de Riel and the other British competitor, Allenby, in the lead with the final leg — the run to come. Based on their points tally, each athlete is given a handicap with the leaders starting on zero. Cook had 49 seconds to make up over a 3km course. It proved no obstacle for the former cross-

country runner as she cut through the field, passing her team-mate and then de Riel with 200 metres to run. Further back was Australian Kitty Chiller, the 35-year-old Melbourne-based sports journalist, who had enjoyed a mixed day. She started well in the shoot and was leading the fencing round at one stage, having won seven out of nine bouts. She had an impressive ride but still had to run off a handicap of 2:20 and finished 14th in the field of 24.

The men's competition produced a dramatic finish as well with towering Russian Dmitry Svatkovsky, the biggest athlete in the field at 188cm and 85kg, coming from fifth spot in the run to win.

He tossed aside any stereotypes of Russian stoicism. As he crossed the line, Svatkovsky punched the air and roared at the crowd. The Olympic title was his, four years after he had finished fourth at Atlanta.

There was not so much joy for Australian Rob McGregor who had hopes of becoming Australia's first medallist in modern pentathlon. After the shooting, he was well placed and needed a good round of fencing to keep him in touch with the leading athletes. It was not to be. He lacked confidence in the elite field and was unable to develop any control.

ATHLETICS

For 50 seconds, Australia held its breath. Cathy Freeman produced a race that stopped the nation to claim the first Australian athletics gold in 12 years. And while world records failed to drop, record crowds mobbed the Olympic stadium throughout the week-long competition.

Above: The winning smiles of the great Michael Johnson and Marion Jones

Opposite page: Cathy Freeman reached out to her family after initially being overwhelmed by her victory in the 400m.

Opening spread: Marion Jones became the first woman to take home five Olympic medals from track and field.

They came and they conquered. And fittingly, to mark the 100th year of female participation in the Olympic Games, the two major stars of the premier sport, track and field, were both women.

America's Marion Jones arrived with her sights set on an unprecedented five gold medals and left with three, plus two bronze. She became the only woman to win five medals in track and field in one Games.

Australia's Cathy Freeman won only one gold, for her signature 400m, and broke no records — but no event in any sport at the Games will be remembered and cherished more by the people of the host nation.

No Olympic Games is all that it might be without a successful and entertaining track and field competition and this was one of the greatest, played out before roaring capacity crowds of around 110,000 every night. Even the first morning session attracted 97,432 fans, another Olympic record.

There were few new entries in record books for the athletes. These were left largely untouched. There were new Olympic records, though no new world marks — but the meet had everything else, including plenty of controversy and some mighty competition.

Jones was certainly the stand-out performer, winning the 100m from Greece's Ekaterina Thanou by the widest margin since Australia's Betty Cuthbert streeted the field in 1952. Jones won the 200m by another huge margin, and then anchored the 400m relay team.

She had to settle for bronze in the long jump, won by Germany's Heiike Dreschler, and in the 100m relay, won by the Bahamas, and when it was all over she said: "Overall I would say it is a successful Games. I wanted to win them all and I still think it's possible."

Jones did all this with great grace under immense pressure, with her husband, world champion shot putter C J Hunter, revealed as a drug cheat just as her colossal campaign was gathering momentum.

There was never any suggestion that she, too, was fuelled by anything more than her enormous talent but that didn't stop the inevitable whispers circulating.

She just smiled her way through it all and kept performing.

However, not even she was the queen of the stadium. Without doubt, that title went to Freeman.

The enduring image of the Games will be her, clad in a space-age green, gold and silver super-hero suit, storming to a victory that grew more and more inevitable as she went through the three preliminary rounds, and then sitting for several minutes on the track, contemplating what she had just achieved.

And then she took off her shoes and broke into a barefoot dance, completing a symbolic tribute to her people, the indigenous Australians, that began when teammate Nova Peris-Kneebone ran barefoot on the first leg of the Torch Relay at Uluru just over 100 days earlier.

That fourth night of the athletics program was a riveting spectacle all round.

America's Michael Johnson became the first man to successfully defend the 400m gold. He also went on to collect another gold medal in the relay.

Ethiopia's Haile Gebrselassie defeated his great rival, Kenyan Paul Tergat, by centimetres in the greatest 10,000m race in Olympic history.

The two blue-riband men's events, the 100m and the 1500m, also produced their customary drama.

America's Maurice Greene promised beforehand that he would win the sprint and duly did so, later doubling up as the anchor runner in the successful relay team.

It was emerging Kenyan, Noah Ngeny, who produced the upset of the meet when he edged out Morocco's Hicham El Gerrouj in the metric mile. El Gerrouj had been virtually unbeatable for five years except at the Olympic Games.

He stumbled and finished last in Atlanta and then made it his life's mission to win in Sydney — but ended up with just another dead dream.

Freeman apart, Australia had a slightly disappointing performance.

The 86 athletes, the biggest Australian team ever, set out in pursuit of five or six medals and a top-five placing among the 199 nations.

Neither target was achieved, with pole vaulter Tatiana Grigoreiva and long jumper Jai Taurima the only other medallists, both collecting silver.

However, officials were pleased that 15 athletes finished in the top eight in their

events and 36 in the top 16; the latter figure represented a 200 per cent increase over a decade.

Taurima's performance was one of the highlights of the meet, partly because he is such an unorthodox character.

He is a party boy who readily admits to drinking and smoking too much, and just before the Games he found himself accused of racism when he described his American rivals as "dribblers" who wouldn't perform well because "dark guys" couldn't handle cool weather.

Those who knew Taurima realised he was only trying to create a bit of media mischief and meant no malice, but he was deeply hurt by the reaction, especially from the Americans.

His own response was to produce three of the four longest jumps of his life to have the gold almost in his hands with just the final round of six jumps to go.

That's when Cuban Ivan Pedroso showed why he is the only man to win three long jump world championships in a row, uncorking a massive final leap of 8.55m to edge Taurima out by 6cm.

Taurima then embarked on a celebration that would surely have won him a gold medal if one was awarded for such activities. His "record" mark was finally leaving the pub at 5.17am.

Undoubtedly, the worst moment for the Australians was when walker Jane Saville was disqualified.

Saville was given her third and final warning for an illegal technique just as she was entering the stadium, clearly in the lead for the 20km gold medal.

Her anguish touched the hearts of the nation when, asked by a TV interviewer what she needed to overcome the disappointment, she replied: "A gun to shoot myself."

There were other disappointments for

Australia, including the baton changing error in the women's 4x100m relay heats and the on-again, off-again appearance of the men's 4x100m relay in the final after a protest by the Italians was upheld against their inclusion. A suspect final baton change in the semis first disqualified the Australian team, but they were reinstated, only to be dumped again after Italy appealed.

The worst moment for anyone else was when Nigerian hurdler Glory Alozie's fiance, a non-Olympic athlete named Hyginus Anugo, was hit by a car and killed just before the Games began.

A devastated Alozie decided to compete to honor his memory and won the silver medal. Other Nigerian runners competed with black tape on their chests.

Relay silver medallist Jude Monye said: "This is in remembrance for our teammate. He is running with us ... his spirit is with us always."

On the final day, the men's marathon also provided a lasting memory for the great Steve Moneghetti.

Moneghetti had been tipped as an outside chance for a medal on the Sydney course, with conditions more suited to him than the incredible heat and humidity of Atlanta or Barcelona.

The Ballarat runner finished a creditable 10th in his final Olympic Games. It was the first time in Moneghetti's long and distinguished career that he had competed at elite level in front of a home crowd. The roar when he entered the stadium was testament to his impact on the Australian sporting public.

In all, 44 countries shared the 139 medals awarded in athletics with the United States leading the way, as usual, with 20.

The US track and field team numbered 128, so perhaps the best performance was from Ethiopia which sent 28 athletes and won eight medals.

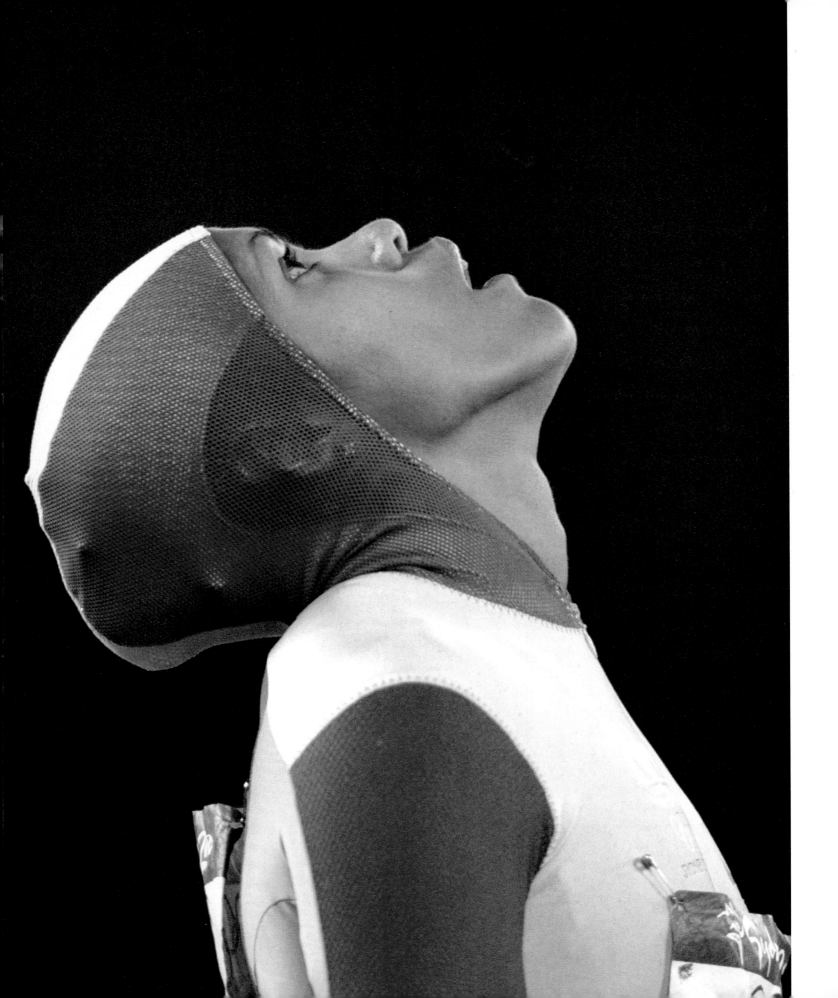

The overwhelming favorite for the 400m, Cathy Freeman wore the expectation of a nation but did not let it faze her.

After wearing a regulation two-piece outfit in the heats and semi-finals, Freeman emerged in the space-age catsuit for the final on a cool Sydney night.

The pace was hot, though, as Freeman convincingly took Australia's first athletics gold since Debbie Flintoff-King won the 400m hurdles in Seoul.

Afterwards, she sat on the track for several minutes, seemingly overwhelmed by the roars of a frenzied home crowd.

Main pictures: The fastest man and woman in the world. Americans Maurice Greene and Marion Jones celebrate seemingly effortless victories in the blue riband 100m sprints.

This page, below left: Jones streets the field in the women's race, with Ekaterina Thanou and Tanya Lawrence fighting it out for the minor placings. Merlene Ottey, Jamaica's 40-year-old sprinter, came in fourth.

This page, below right: Time for rejoicing. Jones embraces her husband CJ Hunter, who needed to buy a ticket for his wife's race when his accreditation was revoked. He continued to deny allegations of drug taking.

Opposite page, below left: Maurice Greene puts his head down in the early stages of his 100m, but easily defeated Ato Boldon and Obadele Thompson.

Opposite page, below middle: Thank you, Australia. Greene launches one of his track spikes into the crowd.

Opposite page, below right: Wagga's Ben Harper, a 20-year-old jeweller, catches Greene's shoe, which was immediately estimated to have a value of more than $100,000. Harper said he would not part with it.

Above: It was just so easy. Marion Jones blitzed the 200m field. Australia had two finalists, Melinda Gainsford-Taylor and Cathy Freeman. While not a placegetter, Gainsford-Taylor was so pleased with her run, she immediately shelved retirement plans.

Below: The Bahamas' 4x100m relay team helped end the party for Marion Jones, the US running into third place.

Opposite page: The winning smile of one of the world's greatest athletes. American Michael Johnson became the first man to win back-to-back gold in the 400m.

Above: Australian, and proud of it. Silver medal winning pole vaulter Tatiana Gregorieva won a new legion of fans.

Right: The great Sergey Bubka won the gold medal for the Soviet Union at Seoul in 1988, but has not had much to celebrate in his three subsequent Olympic campaigns. Now representing Ukraine, he failed to trouble the leaders. Bubka did not go home empty-handed, though; he was elected as an athletes' representative to the International Olympic Committee.

Opposite page, top: Jumping Jai Taurima captivated a nation with his skill and his outrageous way of celebrating silver.

Opposite page, bottom: Maurice Greene powers to his second gold of the Olympic Games, anchoring the 4x100m relay.

Above: Spain's Yago Lamelo flies high in the long jump. He finished with 7.89m to place 12th.

Left: Sergey Kliugin of Russia on his way to winning gold in the high jump.

Opposite page, left: Silver medallist at Atlanta, Louise Currey was forced to withdraw from the javelin after one legal throw because of a knee-injury sustained in the Australian trials.

Opposite page, middle: German great Heike Drechsler took out the long-jump and put paid to Marion Jones' hopes of five gold medals.

Opposite page, right: Australia's Debbie Sosimenko in action in the hammer throw.

Left: A bird's eye view of the men's hurdles heats.

Opposite page, top: The great upset. Moroccan favorite Hicham El Gerrouj is outsprinted by emerging Kenyan Noah Ngeny.

Opposite page, bottom: Hicham El Gerrouj can't believe his misfortune. He has been unbeatable over the distance, except when racing at the Olympic Games. El Gerrouj also tripped and fell during the 1500m in Atlanta.

Above left: Greece's Konstantinos Kenteris can't believe his good fortune after taking gold in the 200m.

Left: A sprint at the end of 10,000m. The incredible Haile Gebreselassie of Ethiopia edged out Kenya's Paul Tergat.

Top: It was an Ethiopian double in the 10,000m, Derartu Tulu claiming gold in the women's race.

Above: Nils Schumann of Germany wins the 800m.

Opposite: The strain shows on two Australian track and field stars, 100m sprinter Matt Shirvington (top) and high jumper Tim Forsyth (bottom).

243

Top: Track and field, including the men's 3000m steeplechase, attracted massive crowds to Sydney's Olympic stadium.

Left: Steve Moneghetti in the main pack going over Sydney Harbour Bridge at the start of the men's marathon.

Opposite page, top: Japan's Naoko Takahashi leads the field heading down to the Sydney CBD in the women's marathon.

Opposite page, bottom left: The smile of a winner. Naoko Takahashi had no peers over the finishing stages of the race.

Opposite page, bottom right: Gezahgne Abera made it a highly-successful Olympic campaign for the Ethiopian track team, winning the men's marathon.

1134 Jane Saville

Above left: Silver medallist Aigars Fadejevs of Latvia cools down after the 50km walk.

Top: Australian Jane Saville leads in the women's 20km walk.

Above: The chief judge puts paid to Saville's dreams of gold in sight of the Olympic stadium (picture courtesy of Channel 7).

Left: Saville is comforted by her fiance, Matt White. Saville's disappointment was heart-rending, but her incredible grace during interviews is an enduring memory of the Games.

Opposite: Do not adjust your book. Walkers reflected in one of the few puddles after a rainy start to the women's 20km event.

EQUESTRIAN

EQUESTRIAN

Australia's incredible record in the gruelling team three-day event continued in fine style at Sydney.

Andrew Hoy, Matt Ryan, Phillip Dutton and Stewart Tinney combined to bring home Australia's third consecutive Olympic gold.

Above: Andrew Hoy's mount, Darien Powers doesn't miss out, with a ribbon on his halter to signify that he, too, is a gold medallist.

Opposite: Making Olympic history. From left, Andrew Hoy, Phillip Dutton, Matt Ryan and Stuart Tinney took Australia's third successive Olympic gold in the Team Three-Day Event.

Opening spread: Australia's four golden horsemen enjoy their lap of honor.

It is not being over-parochial to say that the equestrian program at Horsley Park was a great triumph for Australian horsemanship.

Nor is it overstating the case to say that, throughout the two weeks of competition, high drama was rarely absent from the bushlands west of Sydney where the course was created.

The Australian three-day event team established a record by winning the gold medal for the third consecutive Olympic Games. It rode on the back of an outstanding performance by team captain Andrew Hoy, who himself claimed a third gold on the trot, as it were, and capped it with a silver in the individual event.

One of the greatest head-to-head contests in the sport's history came between Isabell Werth of Germany and the Dutchwoman Anky van Grunsven in the dressage.

That battle ended with van Grunsven reversing the result from Atlanta in 1996 and claiming gold. In the showjumping ring the hot favorite, Rodrigo Pessoa of Brazil, had a tragic finale to his bid when his $5 million mount Baloubet du Rouet refused three times in the final and was disqualified.

Australia's three-day gold was not without controversy. There had been a bitter dispute in Australian horse circles about selection of the team.

There was some crafty politicking from overseas-based riders that annoyed some domestic horsefolk. In the end, three overseas riders were selected: Hoy, Matthew Ryan (both based in England) and US-located Phillip Dutton. Stuart Tinney of NSW made up the four.

Ryan and Dutton both had gold medals from previous Games, and later performances showed the selection was a wise one.

In Atlanta and Barcelona, Australia had won through dominating the cross-country and through Ryan's showjumping.

This time the win was based on a remarkable dressage by Hoy, supported by Tinney and Dutton, and then immaculate cross-country riding by all four.

Pressed by Great Britain, the Australian triumph was in doubt until Tinney rode an ice-cool round in the showjumping, leaving Hoy in the happy position of needing to knock down six rails to lose.

His big, handsome grey Darien Powers was never likely to do that, and soon the four horsemen were riding their traditional laps of honor at full gallop, one of sport's most moving sights.

The other winning horses were Kibah Sandstone, a half-brother to Ryan's winning mount in Barcelona, Jeepster (Tinney) and House Doctor (Dutton).

The United States came in third, led by husband-and-wife team David and Karen O'Connor. O'Connor's faultless showjumping was a precursor to his outstanding win in the individual event,

when Hoy was second and the unlucky New Zealander, the great Mark Todd, third.

Hoy became one of Australia's leading medallists in any sport, and matched Dawn Fraser's feat of winning three consecutive golds in the same event.

More controversy marked the individual and team showjumping with many riders complaining that the surface in the arena was unsatisfactory, even dangerous. They said the topsoil was too loose and the foundation beneath it too firm.

Combined with an unusual degree of difficulty in the fences, the riders had much

trouble in making clear rounds within the set times.

One day was marked by torrential rain, which hardly helped.

Pessoa, son of the legendary Nelson, nonetheless looked secure for a gold until his mount inexplicably baulked at the eighth fence not once but three times.

Pessoa made no excuses, although he later said the horse may have twisted a back nerve at a previous jump.

Other observers thought he might have been spooked by two gaudy mock beachballs alongside the jump.

The disqualification opened the way for a jump-off in which the unheralded Dutchman Jeroen Dubbeldam took gold on Sjiem with the only clear round.

His countryman Albert Voorn had the gold medal sewn up until his mount Lando maddeningly hit the last rail with a trailing hoof.

Another surprising improver, Saudi Arabian Khaled Al Eid on Khashm Al Aan, took bronze. Ironically, he was coached by Nelson Pessoa.

Earlier, Germany had taken the team jumping ahead of Switzerland and Brazil, where Pessoa clinched the bronze, this time with a clear round on Baloubet. The Brazilian took his subsequent disappointment, though, with great dignity.

Werth led Germany to the team medal in dressage, from van Grunsven and her Dutch compatriots with the USA taking bronze. The individual dressage final between Werth, 31, and van Grunsven, 32, was as exciting as this event can ever be.

Finally van Grusven's Bonfire outperformed Werth's Gigolo for a Dutch gold, with another German, Ulla Salzgeber taking bronze.

Despite the worries about the surface, and a glitch in the music during Salzgeber's final performance, the riders left Horsley Park full of praise.

The atmosphere was always both relaxed and gregarious in the superb setting of typical Australian bush in the colours of a Tom Roberts landscape.

Not even the presence of redbelly black snakes, awakening from their winter slumber, worried anyone too much.

The happy sound of bottles of fizz being opened was never far away, and the huge logistical task was astoundingly successful.

Above: Huge crowds turned out at Horsley Park to watch the Three-Day Event.

Opposite, top left: Phillip Dutton doffs his hat in the traditional salute as he finishes the dressage phase on House Doctor.

Opposite, top right: Powering through the cross country course, Matt Ryan and Kibah Sandstone.

Opposite, below left: Stuart Tinney and Jeepster keep Australia's lead alive in the showjumping.

Opposite, below right: Andrew Hoy and the majestic grey Darien Powers take to the cross country course.

Top: Not an English country garden, dressage riders waiting their turn before the start of the Three-Day Team event.
Above: America's Linden Wiseman, on Anderoo, comes to grief.
Left: A sickening moment as Nele Hagener of Germany and her mount Little McMuffin fall at the Orphan steps.

Opposite: Aboriginal art adorned this jump on the cross country course, taken with ease by New Zealand's Mark Todd.

Australia's Amanda Ross narrowly avoids coming to grief at the water jump in the cross country phase of the Three-Day Individual event. She guided her mount Otto Schumaker to 20th place.

Top: Australian Kristy Oatley-Nist won through to the dressage final on Wall Street, finishing ninth.

Above and top right: Dutchman Jeroen Dubbeldam took gold on Sjiem with the only clear round, in a "jump-off" after the disqualification of hot favorite, Rodrigo Pessoa of Brazil.

Right: Reversing the Atlanta result, silver medallist Isabell Werth of Germany and Anky van Grunsven of the Netherlands look old friends on the dressage podium.

Opposite page, top left: Uruguay's Henry Gramajo and mount, Potential come to grief in the individual three-day event.

Opposite page, top right: David O'Connor of the USA held his nerve to take individual three-day event gold.

Opposite page, bottom: Hats off to the great Andrew Hoy and individual three-day event silver.

BASKETBALL

There was no fairytale farewell to Australian legends Andrew Gaze and Michele Timms, who ended their international careers in Sydney. But the Opals and Boomers still showed they are forces in world basketball, each finishing in the top four.

Above: Tears for a champion. Opals captain Michele Timms is embraced by new star Lauren Jackson after the team claimed silver.

Opposite page: Still number one, but pushed all the way. The USA clings to gold.

Opening spread: American forward Shareef Abdur-Rahim tips-in against Russian Nikita Morgunov.

So much is made of the Olympic dream; but it seemed so real for two of Australia's greatest basketballers, Michele Timms and Andrew Gaze, that they could feel it, touch it and taste it.

For Timms, the dream was about a gold medal with the Opals. For Gaze, it was any medal at all with the Boomers. For both of them, Sydney 2000 represented the last chance.

In the end, after outstanding campaigns by the Opals and Boomers, they fell agonisingly short. The Opals won silver and the Boomers finished fourth as Timms and Gaze bade emotional farewells to the international arena.

"How much do I want it?" Timms said before the Olympic final. "Probably more than anything in my life. I could see no greater way to finish than with a gold medal around my neck." Alas for the Opals, the United States continued its domination of women's basketball by adding the 2000 gold medal to those won at the 1996 Olympic Games and the 1998 world championships.

The US, with its cluster of WNBA stars led by Lisa Leslie, beat the Opals, 76-54. But the Americans did not dim the Australian spirit, nor did they dull its shining young star, Lauren Jackson, who capped an excellent tournament with 20 points and 13 rebounds in the gold medal game.

Forward Carla Boyd said: "I'm very proud and it's fantastic to win a silver medal. We won bronze at Atlanta and bronze at the world championships.

"We knew we were better than bronze and hopefully we'll keep getting better and go one more step next time."

That next step was encouraged by not only Jackson, but the efforts of point guard Kristi Harrower, who showed she is world class, and veteran shooting guard Sandy Brondello with her best performance at a major championship.

The bronze medal this time went to emotional and lovable Brazil, which needed overtime to fend off South Korea, the surprise packet of the tournament with its typical Asian-style game of quick ball movement and perimeter shooting that kept a lot of teams off balance.

If the Boomers had been able to snare bronze, it would be have been the most joyous occasion for Gaze and fellow veterans Mark Bradtke, Andrew Vlahov and Luc Longley,

who will follow their captain into international retirement.

After a rocky start, with losses to Canada and Yugoslavia, the Boomers hit back with an amazing win over Russia on Gaze's late three-point bomb, then beat Angola and Spain to make the quarters.

This time, it was Boomers forward Bradtke who made two big free-throws to put them ahead for good against European champion Italy and allowed them to advance to the semi-finals against France.

On the night, though, France was way too good. In the bronze medal game, the Boomers, playing without Longley because of a knee injury, couldn't find form, losing to Lithuania by 18 points.

It was a low end to a good tournament for the Boomers, who had swingman Sam Mackinnon show his maturity and devlopment at this level, as they equalled their best Olympic finish.

"It's a fairly emotional time for us all and in many respects there's a feeling of failure right now," Gaze said. "We'll look back and be disappointed, but still be really proud of our performance."

There were many pundits unimpressed by the performance of the US men's team, even though it won the gold after having to work all the way to the buzzer in the final against the tough and determined French, led by guards Antoine Rigadeau and Laurent Sciarra.

The Americans were perhaps best described as disrespectful to the international game and their opponents with trash talking and gesticulating that might be tolerated, even encouraged, in the NBA, but has no place at the Games.

Though the eventual gold medallist was somewhat predictable, with Vince Carter and Kevin Garnett guilty of both excellent basketball and ridiculous behavior, there was plenty that wasn't.

For example, nobody really thought Canada, paced by supercharged guard Steve Nash, would beat the Boomers on opening night.

Canada kept right on going to beat Yugoslavia and top pool B, only to be upset by France in the quarters.

Who would have thought both Yugoslavia (eighth) and Russia (sixth)

would miss the final four just two years after they fought each other for the 1998 world championship?

Did anybody really think France, after winning just two pool games, would win the silver medal and be within four of the US with only a few minutes to go in the gold-medal game?

That all happened, just as the impossible almost occurred in the semi-finals.

Lithuania went within a basket of beating the US, in what would have been the greatest upset in the history of basketball, and perhaps, in sport.

That game provided the most enthralling moments of the tournament.

Lithuania, the tiny Baltic nation with a proud hoops history, took the mighty and powerful US, the home of basketball, closer to the brink than any NBA-laced team had ever been.

After trailing by 14, Lithuania led with 1:36 to play before the US tied at 80-80.

The drama heightening with every elapsed second, Ramunas Siskauskas stepped to the foul line with 43.3 left for three free-throws.

He knew that was his moment to put Lithuania in a position to gatecrash the Americans' party.

Siskauskas missed two of the three and, in a nutshell, blew it, as the US took the lead and Sarunas Jasikevicius' desperation shot on the buzzer fell short.

The US dodged a bullet, but Lithuania still had plenty of ammunition left for the Boomers in the battle for bronze. It was the second successive Olympic Games that Australia and Lithuania had fought it out for the final medal on offer.

But the dream, for Gaze at least and the other retiring Boomers, was over. Lithuanians Jasikevicius and Saulius Stombergas cranked up the scoring against a flat Australian team, to give the Green Machine its third-straight bronze medal.

Above: Dawn Staley and Teresa Edwards get close and personal to celebrate their second successive gold medal.

Opposite page, top: The Opals proudly show off their silverware.

Opposite page, below left: An intimidating presence inside, America's Yolanda Griffith wrests a rebound.

Opposite page, below right: Michele Timms was severely hampered by a knee injury, for which she underwent further surgery after the Olympic Games. Timms, played limited minutes but took a bigger role in the final after a foot injury to Kristi Harrower. Australia could not match the USA team offensively, playing catch up after the early minutes.

Above left: Who, me? Kevin Garnett can't hide his incredulity at a call during the final against France.

Left: After the medals were handed out, the Americans were more than happy to ham it up for the cameras.

Top: Serious business, Kevin Garnett takes it to the hoop.

Above: Gary Payton fends off the French defence.

Opposite page, main picture: A depressing sight for Australian fans, Lithuania's Saulius Stombergas dunks.

Opposite page, top: Sam Mackinnon vainly tries to spoil a Lithuanian rebound.

Opposite page, middle: Darius Songaila and Mindaugas Timinskas celebrate bronze.

Opposite page, bottom: No medal for five-time Olympian Andrew Gaze.

Above: The support was rabid for the home teams.

Top right: A reverse dunk for Boomer Sam Mackinnon.

Middle: France's Cyril Julian takes a lay-up over Chris Anstey.

Bottom right: The end of Luc Longley's Olympic campaign, helped off the court by Boomers medical staff after a knee injury.

Opposite page: US forces get the nod — the sheer power and talent of America's Vince Carter. The high-priced Team USA, with its bevy of NBA superstars, displayed moments of brilliance but were found wanting by Lithuania and France in the finals. Is their Olympic reign drawing to a close?

Top: Opals guard Annie La Fleur drives past her Russian defender.

Above: There were few headaches for a strong Korean outfit, but Eun-Soon Chung needed an ice-pack in the game against New Zealand.

Right: Into the gold medal game, Australia's Jo Hill celebrated by walking down the court on her hands, while Lauren Jackson applauded.

Above left: Kristi Harrower was up against the tallest threat in women's basketball, 213cm Malgorzata Dydek of Poland.

Left: Go Opals. There was strong home court support for the national team.

Top: Malgorzata Dydek was near-impossible to stop close to the basket.

Above: Katie Smith (USA) tries to defend Russia's Anna Arkhipova.

Left: Farewell ... and thanks. Andrew Gaze, potent as ever at his fifth Games, led the Olympic tournament in scoring

Top: Korean fans were over the top in supporting their women's team.

Below left: Time for some of the Boomers to celebrate with their fans – Andrew Gaze and Chris Anstley move among the faithful.

Opposite page, main picture: France was the surprise packet of the tournament. Centre Frederick Weis, dunking, was part of their strong frontline.

Opposite, below left: Dejan Bodiroga of Yugoslavia was too tough a customer for the Boomers to handle.

Opposite, middle: The long and short of basketball. Mark Dickel of New Zealand is dwarfed by Chinese giant, the 227cm Yao Ming.

Opposite, below right: Italy's Gregor Fucka was no match for American powerhouse Vince Carter.

BOXING

The greats of Cuba proved to be the masters of the boxing ring in Sydney, led by super-heavyweight Felix Savon, who emulated the feats of the great Teofilo Stevenson to claim a third-consecutive gold medal. It was one of four golds claimed by the Latinos.

Above: Cuba's Felix Savon savors the sweet taste of his third gold medal.

Opposite page: American boxer Ricardo Williams kept a picture of his son, Ricardo, laced to his boot. Williams took silver in the light welterweight class.

Felix Savon was not the biggest boxer competing at the Olympic Games but no amateur fighter in the world has such a giant persona or majestic bearing as this enigmatic ring master from Cuba.

He won his third successive heavyweight gold medal in Sydney to join his countryman Teofilo Stevenson and the Hungarian Laszlo Papp as an Olympian with a hat-trick of boxing titles.

But just two days before he entered the history books, Savon sat alone with his melancholy, waiting for an athlete's bus at the back of the Sydney Convention Centre.

The 198cm, 91kg Cuban had suffered a cut under his left eye in his semi-final win over German Sebastian Kober and it was still weeping blood. He also nursed a right hand that, if not broken, is so severely crippled that he now finds even holding a pen difficult.

With a towel draped over his head and his giraffe legs stretched out in a gutter, you could have sworn that instead of whipping Kober, Savon, a shy father of five, had just suffered a humiliating knockout.

The bold young man, who once celebrated gold medals and world championships by clearing all the beer and soft drinks from the press room into his sports bag as mute sportswriters nervously stood by, had been replaced by a sad 33-year-old.

Savon is never comfortable in the spotlight, even though he shined in Sydney, destroying America's reformed armed robber Michael Bennett in the quarter-finals.

He then took gold against ruddy-faced Russian southpaw Sultanahmed Ibzagimov. Savon showed no outward emotion when his hand was raised after the final, only letting his feelings run free backstage, striding out of Hall Three at the Convention Centre, sunglasses hiding his war wounds, and with a smile that could have lit up Havana.

His victory came on a day when the Cubans won four gold medals and again proved their dominance as the premier nation in amateur boxing.

Russia left with two gold medals, as did the emerging boxing power of Kazakhstan. Savon's success followed victories by team-mates Guillermo Rigondeaux (54kg), Mario Kindelan (60kg) and Jorge Gutierrez (71kg), all southpaws and all superb in victory.

The four golden boys were anticipating a hero's welcome home from Fidel Castro and 11 million of their grateful countrymen.

France was also celebrating the success of 48kg champion Brahim Asloum, their first Olympic boxing gold since 1936.

With his hair tinted red, white and blue, Asloum had been the giant-killer of the lightest division.

Asloum eliminated the two gold medal favorites, Maikro Romero of Cuba and the "Hawaiian Punch" Brian Viloria of the USA. He then outpointed the shortest fighter in Sydney, Spain's 150cm southpaw Rafael Lozano.

Fresh-faced journalist Oleg Saitov created his own headlines, repeating his Atlanta triumph in the 67kg division to outscore Ukrainian Sergey Dotsenko.

Saitov has no imposing physique and probably hits a keyboard harder than he does opponents.

But he is a master boxer with an immaculate defence and showed that he has the heart of a champion in winning his semi-final against the rugged Dorel Simion, who is just about the most frightening thing out of Romania since Dracula.

Simion's brother Marian, the world champ, lost a close decision in his final and went home with silver on a day when Britain celebrated its first Olympic boxing gold in 32 years.

Britain's 198cm and 110kg champion, Audley Harrison, defied a damaged left hand to win the super-heavyweight gold and assure himself of a multi-million dollar contract to fight professionally.

The highly touted Americans would have been disappointed to go home without a gold medal for the first time in 52 years after their two finalists, Ricardo Williams and Rocky Juarez, lost points decisions.

As for Australia, many of their boxers were beaten before they started by fierce infighting in the team.

The sticking point was the methods of coach Bodo Andreass, a former East German boxer, who doesn't pull his punches.

Brisbane's Richie Rowles (71kg) said Andreass was a coach who demanded respect but gave none in return. Rowles pounded Dominican Juan Cabrera but looked a totally different fighter in losing to German Adnan Catic.

Like Rowles, Toowoomba lightweight Michael Katsidis (60kg) was not on speaking terms with the national coach for much of his preparation.

Katsidis battered Brazilian brewery worker

Agnaldo Magalhaes but then lost a 9-7 points decision to Kazakhstan tax expert Nurzhan Karimzhanov.

Despite the controversies, Andreass had his supporters, too.

One of them, Queensland middleweight (75kg) Paul Miller, lost to bronze medallist Vugar Alekperov by a single point.

Perth flyweight (51kg) Erle Wiltshire was treated to a boxing lesson from French bronze medallist Jerome Thomas, an anatomy student with a deformed fist and one arm shorter than the other.

Maroochydore teenager Justin Kane (54kg), fighting to win a medal for his father who has throat cancer, reached the quarter-finals by defeating Thailand's Sontoya Wongprates but dipped out against Ukrainian Serguey Daniltchenko.

Perth's Danny Green (81kg) pounded out Brazilian Laudelino Barros but could not counter the tactical brilliance of Moscow Army officer Alexander Lebziak, a mauler who finally won a gold medal after coming up short at two previous Games.

Adelaide featherweight James Swan (57kg) announced he was turning pro after being outpointed by Brazilian Valdemir dos Santos Pereira.

Welterweight Daniel Geale, from Lilydale near Launceston, came up short in a decision to Italian-based Leonard Bundu, a native of Sierra Leone.

Henry Collins (63.5kg), an apprentice cabinet maker from Alice Springs, was outclassed in his first fight by America's silver medallist, Ricardo Williams Jnr.

Australia's lightest fighter, 48kg teenager Bradley Hore, was knocked out even before he got to throw a punch when he could not make the weight limit despite spending eight hours in a sauna smeared in honey.

Hore was inconsolable after failing to make the weight, and was forced to leave the athlete's village.

It was the cruellest blow of the Games.

Above: A badly cut eye did not hamper Felix Savon (red) of Cuba in his gold medal bout against Sultanahmed Ibzagimov of Russia.

Left: Blue-haired Justin Kane of Australia performs his trademark backflip after a victory. Sadly, for the home team, wins proved infrequent.

Opposite page: Ukraine fighter Sergey Dotsenko lifts 67kg class gold medallist, Russia's Oleg Saitov.

CLOSING CEREMONY

It was time to say goodbye. The Closing Ceremony of the Sydney 2000 Olympic Games showcased the best of Australia, from its music and culture to its world-famous icons. In contrast to the formality 17 days earlier, it was a carefree and exhilarating night.

Above: Ian Thorpe proudly led the Australian team with the flag.

Opposite page, top: Kylie Minogue whipped the crowd into a frenzy when she sang "Dancing Queen".
Opposite page, bottom: An Australian icon, the thong, ferried Minogue into the stadium and was then warmly embraced by the athletes of the world.

Opening spread: The moment when Sydney bade farewell to the athletes of the world.

The words that all Australia had been waiting for were uttered with gusto. International Olympic Committee president Juan Antonio Samaranch, presiding over his final Games before retirement, spoke with conviction.

It was official — the Sydney 2000 Olympic Games were the best ever. Samaranch's words were punctuated by an exuberant Closing Ceremony.

The ceremony was a celebration of Australian culture, focusing on the icons Australia has given to the world. There were thongs, surf lifesavers, Hills hoists. There was Kylie Minogue, Greg Norman, Paul Hogan and Elle Macpherson. Then, we saw Bananas in Pyjamas — they sounded so much more exotic when introduced in French.

The performers kept coming — Minogue had the honor of two songs, and she was joined on stage by Jimmy Barnes, INXS with Jon Stevens out front, Midnight Oil, with the word "sorry" emblazoned in white over their black outfits, comment on the reconcilation process brought into focus by these Games.

It was the best, and the crowd loved it.

The athletes, all the pressure of the previous 17 days stripped from their faces, channelled their considerable energy into singing and dancing. Conga lines formed around the arena — and there were plenty more besides among the capacity stadium.

During the few speeches, for there was a solemn side to the evening as well, it was fitting that Samaranch and the SOCOG dignitaries paid tribute to the thousands of volunteers who had given so generously of themselves to make Sydney 2000 a rousing success. Many volunteers were able to share in the closing ceremony after SOCOG made a rare public relations coup, donating unsold tickets to them.

It was 17 days of passion and fire, of disappointment and triumph, of despair and the highest of heights.

It was the Olympic movement, faster, higher, stronger than ever before. It was a celebration of the world, as well as everything uniquely Australian.

For 199 nations, it was an intensely unifying experience. For the millions who attended or watched, it was the sporting highlight of their lives.

Top: The Bondi lifesavers had a huge impact on the hometown crowd.

Above: Bananas in Pyjamas were part of the parade of icons.

Above right: An invention Australia gave the world, the Hills Hoist.

Opposite page, top: Throw another one on the barbie. Giant prawns on bikes brought back memories of the kangaroos from the Atlanta closing ceremony.

Opposite, below left and right: It was a Mambo kind of night. Giant inflatables of Reg Mombassa's art figures roamed among the crowd.

AFG	Afghanistan	BLR	Belarus	CPV	Cape Verde	DJI	Djibouti	GER	Germany	IRI	Iran
ALB	Albania	BEL	Belgium	CAY	Cayman Islands	DMA	Dominica	GHA	Ghana	IRQ	Iraq
ALG	Algeria	BIZ	Belize	CAF	Central African Republic	DOM	Dominican Republic	GBR	Great Britain	IRL	Ireland
ASA	American Samoa	BEN	Benin	CHA	Chad	IOA	East Timor	GRE	Greece	ISR	Israel
AND	Andorra	BER	Bermuda	CHI	Chile	ECU	Ecuador	GRN	Grenada	ITA	Italy
ANG	Angola	BHU	Bhutan	CHN	China	EGY	Egypt	GUM	Guam	JAM	Jamaica
ANT	Antigua and Barbuda	BOL	Bolivia	COL	Colombia	ESA	El Salvador	GUA	Guatemala	JPN	Japan
ARG	Argentina	BIH	Bosnia and Herzegovina	COM	Comoros	GEQ	Equatorial Guinea	GUI	Guinea	JOR	Jordan
ARM	Armenia	BOT	Botswana	CGO	Congo	ERI	Eritrea	GBS	Guinea-Bissau	KAZ	Kazakhstan
ARU	Aruba	BRA	Brazil	COK	Cook Islands	EST	Estonia	GUY	Guyana	KEN	Kenya
AUS	Australia	BRU	Brunei Darussalam	CRC	Costa Rica	ETH	Ethiopia	HAI	Haiti	PRK	Democratic People's
AUT	Austria	BUL	Bulgaria	CIV	Cote d'Ivoire	FIJ	Fiji	HON	Honduras		Republic of Korea (North Korea)
AZE	Azerbaijan	BUR	Burkina Faso	CRO	Croatia	FIN	Finland	HKG	Hong Kong	KOR	Republic of Korea
BAH	Bahamas	BDI	Burundi	CUB	Cuba	FRA	France	HUN	Hungary		(South Korea)
BRN	Bahrain	CAM	Cambodia	CYP	Cyprus	GAB	Gabon	ISL	Iceland	KUW	Kuwait
BAN	Bangladesh	CMR	Cameroon	CZE	Czech Republic	GAM	Gambia	IND	India	KGZ	Kyrgyzstan
BAR	Barbados	CAN	Canada	DEN	Denmark	GEO	Georgia	INA	Indonesia	LAO	Laos

LAT	Latvia	MEX	Mexico	NOR	Norway	SKN	Saint Kitts and Nevis	ESP	Spain	TUR	Turkey
LIB	Lebanon	FSM	Micronesia	OMA	Oman	LCA	Saint Lucia	SRI	Sri Lanka	UGA	Uganda
LES	Lesotho	MDA	Moldova	PAK	Pakistan	VIN	Saint Vincent	SUD	Sudan	UKR	Ukraine
LBR	Liberia	MON	Monaco	PLW	Palau		and the Grenadines	SUR	Surinam	UAE	United Arab Emirates
LBA	Libya	MGL	Mongolia	PLE	Palestine	SAM	Samoa	SWZ	Swaziland	USA	United States of America
LIE	Liechtenstein	MAR	Morocco	PAN	Panama	SMR	San Marino	SWE	Sweden	URU	Uruguay
LTU	Lithuania	MOZ	Mozambique	PNG	Papua New Guinea	STP	Sao Tome and Principe	SUI	Switzerland	UZB	Uzbekistan
LUX	Luxembourg	MYA	Myanmar	PAR	Paraguay	KSA	Saudi Arabia	SYR	Syria	VAN	Vanuatu
MKD	Macedonia	NAM	Namibia	PER	Peru	SEN	Senegal	TPE	Taiwan	VEN	Venezuela
MAD	Madagascar	NRU	Nauru	PHI	Philippines	SEY	Seychelles	TJK	Tajikistan	VIE	Vietnam
MAW	Malawi	NEP	Nepal	POL	Poland	SLE	Sierra Leone	TAN	Tanzania	IVB	Virgin Islands (UK)
MAS	Malaysia	NED	Netherlands	POR	Portugal	SIN	Singapore	THA	Thailand	IVR	Virgin Islands (US)
MDV	Maldives	AHO	Netherlands Antilles	PUR	Puerto Rico	SVK	Slovakia	TOG	Togo	YEM	Yemen
MLI	Mali	NZL	New Zealand	QAT	Qatar	SLO	Slovenia	TGA	Tonga	YUG	Yugoslavia
MLT	Malta	NCA	Nicaragua	ROM	Romania	SOL	Solomon Islands	TRI	Trinidad and Tobago	ZAI	Zaire
MTN	Mauritania	NIG	Niger	RUS	Russia	SOM	Somalia	TUN	Tunisia	ZAM	Zambia
MRI	Mauritius	NGR	Nigeria	RWA	Rwanda	RSA	South Africa	TKM	Turkemistan	ZIM	Zimbabwe

SYDNEY 2000 OLYMPIC GAMES
MEDAL TALLY

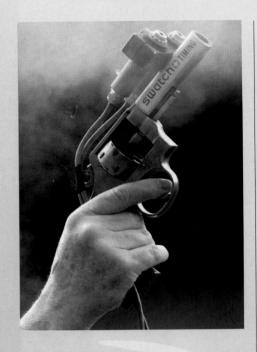

	G	S	B	T
USA	39	25	33	97
Russian Federation	32	28	28	88
China	28	16	15	59
AUSTRALIA	16	25	17	58
Germany	14	17	26	57
France	13	14	11	38
Italy	13	8	13	34
Netherlands	12	9	4	25
Cuba	11	11	7	29
Great Britain	11	10	7	28
Romania	11	6	9	26
Korea	8	9	11	28
Hungary	8	6	3	17
Poland	6	5	3	14
Japan	5	8	5	18
Bulgaria	5	6	2	13
Greece	4	6	3	13
Sweden	4	5	3	12
Norway	4	3	3	10
Ethiopia	4	1	3	8
Ukraine	3	10	10	23
Kazakhstan	3	4	0	7
Belarus	3	3	11	17
Canada	3	3	8	14
Spain	3	3	5	11
Islamic Republic of Iran	3	0	1	4
Turkey	3	0	1	4
Czech Republic	2	3	3	8
Kenya	2	3	2	7
Denmark	2	3	1	6
Finland	2	1	1	4
Austria	2	1	0	3
Lithuania	2	0	3	5
Azerbaijan	2	0	1	3
Slovenia	2	0	0	2
Switzerland	1	6	2	9
Indonesia	1	3	2	6
Slovakia	1	3	1	5
Mexico	1	2	3	6
Algeria	1	1	3	5

	G	S	B	T
Uzbekistan	1	1	2	4
Latvia	1	1	1	3
Yugoslavia	1	1	1	3
Bahamas	1	1	0	2
New Zealand	1	0	3	4
Estonia	1	0	2	3
Thailand	1	0	2	3
Croatia	1	0	1	2
Cameroon	1	0	0	1
Colombia	1	0	0	1
Mozambique	1	0	0	1
Brazil	0	6	6	12
Jamaica	0	4	3	7
Nigeria	0	3	0	3
Belgium	0	2	3	5
South Africa	0	2	3	5
Argentina	0	2	2	4
Morocco	0	1	4	5
Chinese Taipei	0	1	4	5
DPR Korea	0	1	3	4
Saudi Arabia	0	1	1	2
Republic of Moldova	0	1	1	2
Trinidad and Tobago	0	1	1	2
Ireland	0	1	0	1
Uruguay	0	1	0	1
Vietnam	0	1	0	1
Georgia	0	0	6	6
Costa Rica	0	0	2	2
Portugal	0	0	2	2
Armenia	0	0	1	1
Barbados	0	0	1	1
Chile	0	0	1	1
India	0	0	1	1
Iceland	0	0	1	1
Israel	0	0	1	1
Kyrgyzstan	0	0	1	1
Kuwait	0	0	1	1
FYR Macedonia	0	0	1	1
Qatar	0	0	1	1
Sri Lanka	0	0	1	1

ARCHERY

MEN

INDIVIDUAL

G	Simon Fairweather	AUS
S	Victor Wunderle	USA
B	Wieste van Alten	NED
24	Scott Hunter-Russell	AUS
36	Matt Gray	AUS

TEAM

G	South Korea	
S	Italy	
B	United States	
12	Australia – Matthew Gray, Simon Fairweather, Scott Hunter-Russell	

WOMEN

INDIVIDUAL

G	Mi-Jin Yun	KOR
S	Kim Nam-Soon	KOR
B	Kim Soo-Nyung	KOR
11	Michelle Tremelling	AUS
19	Melissa Jennison	AUS
22	Kate Fairweather	AUS

TEAM

G	South Korea	
S	Ukraine	
B	Germany	
9	Australia - Kate Fairweather, Melissa Jennison, Michelle Tremelling	

ATHLETICS

MEN

100M

G	Maurice Greene	USA
S	Ato Boldon	TRI
B	Obadele Thompson	BAR
SF	Matt Shirvington	AUS
DNQ	Patrick Johnson	AUS
DNQ	Paul di Bella	AUS

200M

G	Konstantinos Kenteris	GRE
S	Darren Campbell	GBR
B	Ato Boldon	TRI
DNQ	Patrick Johnson	AUS
DNS	Matt Shirvington	AUS
DNQ	Darryl Wohlsen	AUS

400M

G	Michael Johnson	USA
S	Alvin Harrison	USA
B	Gregory Haughton	JAM
SF	Patrick Dwyer	AUS
SF	Casey Vincent	AUS
DNF	Daniel Batman	AUS

800M

G	Nils Schumann	GER
S	Wilson Kipketer	DEN
B	Aissa Djabir Said-Guerni	ALG
SF	Grant Cremer	AUS
DNQ	Kris McCarthy	AUS

1500M

G	Noah Ngeny	KEN
S	Hicham El Guerrouj	MAR
B	Bernard Lagat	KEN
DNQ	Nick Howarth	AUS

3000M STEEPLECHASE

G	Reuben Kosgei	KEN
S	Wilson Boit Kipketer	KEN
B	Ali Ezzine	MAR
DNQ	Chris Unthank	AUS

5000M

G	Millon Wolde	ETH
S	Ali Saidi-Sief	ALG
B	Brahim Lahlafi	MAR
12	Mizan Mehari	AUS
DNQ	Craig Mottram	AUS
DNQ	Michael Power	AUS

10,000M

G	Haile Gebrselassie	ETH
S	Paul Tergat	KEN
B	Assefa Mezgebu	ETH
11	Sisay Bezabeh	AUS
14	Shaun Creighton	AUS

MARATHON

G	Gezahgne Abera	ETH
S	Eric Wainaina	KEN
B	Tesfaye Tola	ETH
10	Steve Moneghetti	AUS
28	Rod de Highden	AUS
66	Lee Troop	AUS

110M HURDLES

G	Anier Garcia	CUB
S	Terrence Trammell	USA
B	Mark Crear	USA
SF	Kyle Vander-Kuyp	AUS

400M HURDLES

G	Angelo Taylor	USA
S	Hadi Souan Somayli	KSA
B	Llewellyn Herbert	RSA
SF	Blair Young	AUS
DNQ	Rohan Robinson	AUS
DNQ	Matthew Beckenham	AUS

4X100M RELAY

G	United States	
S	Brazil	
B	Cuba	
DSQ	Australia - Matt Shirvington, Paul di Bella, Darryl Wohlsen, Patrick Johnson (Damien Marsh, Kieren Noonan)	

4X400M RELAY

G	United States	
S	Nigeria	
B	Jamaica	
8	Australia - Brad Jamieson, Blair Young, Michael Hazel, Patrick Dwyer, (Daniel Batman, Casey Vincent)	

20KM WALK

G	Robert Korzeniowski	POL
S	Noe Hernandez	MEX
B	Vladimir Andreyev	RUS
8	Nathan Deakes	AUS
10	Nicholas A'Hern	AUS
25	Dion Russell	AUS

50KM WALK

G	Robert Korzeniowski	POL
S	Aigars Fadejevs	LAT
B	Joel Sanchez	MEX
6	Nathan Deakes	AUS
27	Dion Russell	AUS
34	Duane Cousins	AUS

HIGH JUMP

G	Sergey Kliugin	RUS
S	Javier Sotomayor	CUB
B	Abderrahmane Hammad	ALG
DNQ	Tim Forsyth	AUS

LONG JUMP

G	Ivan Pedroso	CUB
S	Jai Taurima	AUS
B	Roman Schurenko	UKR
6	Peter Burge	AUS

TRIPLE JUMP

G	Jonathan Edwards	GBR
S	Yoel Garcia	CUB
B	Denis Kapustin	RUS
10	Andrew Murphy	AUS

POLE VAULT

G	Nick Hysong	USA
S	Lawrence Johnson	USA
B	Maksim Tarasov	RUS
5	Viktor Chistiakov	AUS
5	Dmitry Markov	AUS
DNQ	Paul Burgess	AUS

SHOT PUT

G	Arsi Harju	FIN
S	Adam Nelson	USA
B	John Godina	USA
29	Justin Anlezark	AUS

DISCUS

G	Virgilijus Alekna	LTU
S	Lars Riedel	GER
B	Frantz Kruger	RSA

HAMMER THROW

G	Szymon Ziolkowski	POL
S	Nicola Vizzoni	ITA
B	Igor Astapkovich	BLR
28	Stuart Rendell	AUS

JAVELIN

G	Jan Zelezny	CZE
S	Steve Backley	GBR
B	Sergey Makarov	RUS
DNQ	Andrew Martin	AUS
DNQ	Adrian Hatcher	AUS
DNQ	Andrew Currey	AUS

DECATHLON

G	Erik Nool	EST
S	Roman Sebrie	CZE
B	Chris Huffins	USA
DNF	Scott Ferrier	AUS

WOMEN

100M

G	Marion Jones	USA
S	Ekaterini Thanou	GRE
B	Tanya Lawrence	JAM
SF	Melinda Gainsford-Taylor	AUS
DNQ	Lauren Hewitt	AUS

200M

G	Marion Jones	USA
S	Pauline Davis-Thompson	BAH
B	Susanthika Jayasinghe	SRI
6	Melinda Gainsford-Taylor	AUS
7	Cathy Freeman	AUS
SF	Lauren Hewitt	AUS

400M

G	Cathy Freeman	AUS
S	Lorraine Graham	JAM
B	Katharine Merry	GBR
SF	Nova Peris-Kneebone	AUS
DNQ	Lee Naylor	AUS

800M

G	Maria Mutola	MOZ
S	Stephanie Graf	AUT
B	Kelly Holmes	GBR
SF	Tamsyn Lewis	AUS
DNQ	Susan Andrews	AUS

1500M

G	Nouria Merah-Benida	ALG
S	Violeta Szekely	ROM
B	Gabriela Szabo	ROM
SF	Margaret Crowley	AUS
SF	Georgie Clarke	AUS
DNQ	Sarah Jamieson	AUS

5000M

G	Gabriela Szabo	ROM
S	Sonia O'Sullivan	IRL
B	Gete Wami	ETH
DNQ	Benita Willis	AUS
DNQ	Anne Cross	AUS
DNQ	Kate Richardson	AUS

10,000M

G	Derartu Tulu	ETH
S	Gete Wami	ETH
B	Fernanda Ribeiro	POR
DNQ	Clair Fearnley	AUS
DNQ	Kylie Risk	AUS
DNQ	Natalie Harvey	AUS

MARATHON

G	Naoko Takahashi	JPN
S	Lidia Simon	ROM
B	Joyce Chepchumba	KEN
11	Kerryn McCann	AUS
35	Sue Hobson	AUS
DNF	Nicole Carroll	AUS

100M HURDLES

G	Olga Shishigina	KAZ
S	Glory Alozie	NGR
B	Melissa Morrison	USA
DNQ	Deborah Edwards	AUS

400M HURDLES

G	Irina Privalova	RUS
S	Deon Hemmings	JAM
B	Nouzha Bidouane	MAR
DNQ	Jana Pittman	AUS
DNQ	Lauren Poetschka	AUS
DNQ	Stephanie Price	AUS

4X100M RELAY

G	Bahamas	
S	Jamaica	
B	United States	

DNF Australia - Elly Hutton, Lauren Hewitt, Sharon Cripps, Melinda Gainsford-Taylor

4X400M RELAY

G	United States	
S	Jamaica	
B	Russian Federation	

5 Australia – Nova Peris-Kneebone, Tamsyn Lewis, Melinda Gainsford-Taylor, Cathy Freeman, (Susan Andrews, Jana Pittman)

20KM WALK

G	Liping Wang	CHN
S	Kjersti Plaetzer	NOR
B	Maria Vasco	ESP
7	Kerry Saxby-Junna	AUS
39	Lisa Sheridan-Paolini	AUS
DSQ	Jane Saville	AUS

HIGH JUMP

G	Yelena Yelesina	RUS
S	Hestrie Cloete	RSA
B	Kajsa Bergqvist	SWE
B	Oana Manuela	ROM
32	Alison Inverarity	AUS

LONG JUMP

G	Heike Drechsler	GER
S	Fiona May	ITA
B	Marion Jones	USA
16	Bronwyn Thompson	AUS

TRIPLE JUMP

G	Tereza Marinova	BUL
S	Tatyana Lebedeva	RUS
B	Olena Hovorova	UKR

POLE VAULT

G	Stacy Dragila	USA
S	Tatiana Grigorieva	AUS
B	Vala Flosadottir	ISL
DNQ	Emma George	AUS

SHOT PUT

G	Yanina Korolchik	BLR
S	Larisa Peleshenko	RUS
B	Astrid Kumbernuss	GER

DISCUS

G	Ellina Zvereva	BLR
S	Anastasia Kelesidou	GRE
B	BIrina Yatchenko	BLR
8	Lisa-Marie Vizaniari	AUS
DNQ	Alison Lever	AUS
DNQ	Daniela Costian	AUS

HAMMER THROW

G	Kamila Skolimowska	POL
S	Olga Kuzenkova	RUS
B	Kristen Muenchow	GER
5	Debbie Sosimenko	AUS
21	Karyne Perkins	AUS

JAVELIN

G	Trine Hattestad	NOR
S	Mirella Maniani-Tzelili	GRE
B	Osleidys Menendez	CUB
17	Jo Stone	AUS
31	Louise Currey	AUS

HEPTATHLON

G	Denise Lewis	GBR
S	Yelena Prokhorova	RUS
B	Natalya Sazanovich	BLR
10	Jane Jamieson	AUS

BADMINTON

MEN

SINGLES

G	Xinpeng Ji	CHN
S	Hendrawan	INA
B	Xuanze Xia	CHN
R2	Rio Suryana	AUS

DOUBLES

G	Gunawan/Wijaya	INA
S	Lee/Yoo	KOR
B	Ha/Kim	KOR

R1 Australia - Peter Blackburn/ David Bamford

WOMEN

SINGLES

G	Zhichao Gong	CHN
S	Camilla Martin	DEN
B	Zhaoying Ye	CHN
R2	Rhonda Cator	AUS
R2	Rayoni Head	AUS
R1	Kellie Lucas	AUS

DOUBLES

G	Fei Ge/Jun Gu	CHN
S	Nanyan Huang/Wei Yang	CHN
B	Ling Gao/Yiyuan Qin	CHN

R1 Australia - Rhonda Cator/ Amanda Hardy, Rayoni Head/Kellie Lucas

MIXED

DOUBLES

G	Gao/Zhang	CHN
S	Kusharyanto/Timur	INA
B	Archer/Goode	GBR

R1 Australia - David Bamford/ Amanda Hardy, Peter Blackburn/ Rhonda Cator, Rio Suryana/ Kellie Lucas

BASEBALL

G	United States	
S	Cuba	
B	South Korea	

7 Australia – Craig Anderson, Grant Balfour, Tom Becker, Shayne Bennett, Matthew Buckley, Adam Burton, Clayton Byrne, Cameron Cairncross, Trent Durrington, Paul Gonzalez, Mark Hutton, Ron Johnson, Grant McDonald, Adrian Meagher, Michael Moyle, David Nilsson, Glenn Reeves, Brett Roneberg, Chris Snelling, Brad Thomas, Gary White, Glenn Williams

BASKETBALL

MEN

G	United States	
S	France	
B	Lithuania	

4 Australia – Chris Anstey, Mark Bradtke, Martin Cattalini, Andrew Gaze, Ricky Grace, Shane Heal, Luc Longley, Sam Mackinnon, Brett Maher, Paul Rogers, Jason Smith, Andrew Vlahov

WOMEN

G	United States	
S	Australia – Carla Boyd,	

Sandy Brondello, Trish Fallon, Michelle Griffiths, Kristi Harrower, Jo Hill, Lauren Jackson, Annie La Fleur, Shelley Sandie, Rachael Sporn, Michele Timms, Jenny Whittle

B	Brazil	

BOXING

48KG

G	Brahim Asloum	FRA
S	Rafael Lozano Munoz	ESP
B	Maikro Romero Esquirol	CUB
B	Un Chol Kim	PRK
DNC	Bradley Hore	AUS

51KG

G	Wijan Ponlid	THA
S	Bulat Jumadilov	KAZ
B	Vladimir Sidorenko	UKR
B	Jerome Thomas	FRA
R1	Erle Wiltshire	AUS

54KG

G	Guillermo Rigondeaux Ortiz	CUB
S	Raimkoul Malakhbekov	RUS
B	Serguey Daniltchenko	UKR
B	Clarence Vinson	USA
QF	Justin Kane	AUS

57KG

G	Bekzat Sattarkhanov	KAZ
S	Ricardo Juarez	USA
B	Tahar Tamsamani	MAR
B	Kamil Dzamalutdinov	RUS
R1	James Swan	AUS

60KG

G	Mario Kindelan	CUB
S	Andriy Kotelnyk	UKR
B	Cristian Bejarano Benitez	MEX
B	Alexandr Maletin	RUS
R2	Michael Katsidis	AUS

63.5KG

G	Mahamadkadyz Abdullaev	UZB
S	Ricardo Williams	USA
B	Mohamed Allalou	ALG
B	Diogenes Luna Martinez	CUB
R1	Henry Collins	AUS

67KG

G	Oleg Saitov	RUS
S	Sergey Dotsenko	UKR
B	Vitalii Grusac	MDA
B	Dorel Simion	ROM
R2	Daniel Geale	AUS

71KG

G	Yermakhan Ibraimov	KAZ
S	Marin Simion	ROM
B	Jermain Taylor	USA
B	Pornchai Thongburan	THA
R2	Richard Rowles	AUS

75KG

G	Jorge Gutierrez	CUB
S	Gaidarbek Gaidarbekov	RUS
B	Vugar Alekperov	AZE
B	Zsolt Erdei	HUN
R2	Paul Miller	AUS

81KG

G	Alexander Lebziak	RUS
S	Rudolf Kraj	CZE
B	Andri Fedtchouk	UKR
B	Sergei Mikhailov	UZB
R2	Daniel Green	AUS

91KG

G	Felix Savon	CUB
S	Sultanahmed Ibzagimov	RUS
B	Vladimir Tchantouria	GEO
B	Sebastian Kober	GER

91+KG

G	Audley Harrison	GBR
S	Mukhtarkhan Dildabekov	KAZ
B	Paolo Vidoz	ITA
B	Rustam Saidov	UZE

CANOE/KAYAK

MEN

CANOE SINGLES 500M

G	Gyorgy Kolonics	HUN
S	Maxim Opalev	RUS
B	Andreas Dittmer	GER

CANOE SINGLES 1000M

G	Andreas Dittmer	GER
S	Ledys Frank Balceiro	CUB
B	Steve Giles	CAN

CANOE PAIRS 500M

G	Hungary	
S	Poland	
B	Romania	

CANOE PAIRS 1000M

G	Romania	
S	Cuba	
B	Germany	

CANOE SINGLES SLALOM (WHITEWATER)

G	Tony Estanguet	FRA
S	Michal Martikan	SVK
B	Juraj Mincik	SVK
9	Robin Bell	AUS

CANOE PAIRS SLALOM (WHITEWATER)

G	Pavol Hochschorner/ Peter Hochschorner	SVK
S	Krzysztof Kolomanski/ Michal Staniszewski	POL
B	Marek Jiras/ Thomas Mader	CZE
11	Kai Swoboda/ Andrew Farrance	AUS

KAYAK SINGLES 500M

G	Knut Holmann	NOR
S	Petar Merkov	BUL
B	Michael Kolganov	ISR
SF	Nathan Baggaley	AUS

KAYAK SINGLES 1000M

G	Knut Holmann	NOR
S	Petar Merkov	BUL
B	Tim Brabants	GBR
SF	Clint Robinson	AUS

KAYAK PAIRS 500M

G	Hungary	
S	Australia Andrew Trim/Daniel Collins	
B	Germany	

KAYAK PAIRS 1000M

G	Italy	
S	Sweden	
B	Hungary	
SF	Australia Brian Morton/Luke Young	

KAYAK FOURS 1000M

G	Hungary	
S	Germany	
B	Poland	
SF	Australia Ross Chaffer, Shane Suska, Peter Scott, Cameron McFadzean	

KAYAK SINGLES SLALOM (WHITEWATER)

G	Thomas Schmidt	GER
S	Paul Ratcliffe	GBR
B	Pierpaolo Ferrazzi	ITA
21	John Wilkie	AUS

WOMEN

KAYAK SINGLES 500M

G	Josefa Idem Guerrini	ITA
S	Caroline Brunet	CAN
B	Katrin Borchert	AUS

KAYAK PAIRS 500M

G	Germany	
S	Hungary	
B	Poland	
6	Australia Anna Wood/Katrin Borchert	

KAYAK FOURS 500M

G	Germany	
S	Hungary	
B	Romania	
SF	Australia – Yanda Nossiter, Kerri Randle, Amanda Simper, Shelley Oates-Wilding	

KAYAK SINGLES SLALOM (WHITEWATER)

G	Stepanki Hilgertova	CZE
S	Brigitte Guibal	FRA
B	Anne-Lise Bardet	FRA
8	Danielle Woodward	AUS

CYCLING

MEN

ROAD RACE

G	Jan Ullrich	GER
S	Alexandr Vinokourov	KAZ
B	Andreas Kioeden	GER
19	Robbie McEwen	AUS
30	Henk Vogels	AUS
77	Stuart O'Grady	AUS
DNF	Scott McGrory	AUS
DNF	Matthew White	AUS

INDIVIDUAL TIME TRIAL (ROAD)

G	Viacheslav Ekimov	RUS
S	Jan Ullrich	GER
B	Lance Armstrong	USA
19	Nathan O'Neill	AUS

1KM TIME TRIAL (TRACK)

G	Jason Queally	GBR
S	Stefan Nimke	GER
B	Shane Kelly	AUS

4000M INDIVIDUAL PURSUIT

G	Robert Batko	GER
S	Jens Lehmann	GER
B	Brad McGee	AUS
9	Luke Roberts	AUS

4000M TEAM PURSUIT

G	Germany	
S	Ukraine	
B	Great Britain	
5	Australia - Brett Aitken, Graeme Brown, Brad McGee, Michael Rogers, (Brett Lancaster)	

SPRINT

G	Marty Nothstein	USA
S	Florian Rousseau	FRA
B	Jens Fiedler	GER
7	Sean Eadie	AUS
12	Darryn Hill	AUS

OLYMPIC SPRINT

G	France	
S	Great Britain	
B	Australia - Gary Niewand, Sean Eadie, Darryn Hill	

POINTS RACE

G	Juan Llaneras	ESP
S	Milton Wynants	URU
B	Alexey Markov	RUS
10	Stuart O'Grady	AUS

MADISON

G	Australia Scott McGory/Brett Aitken	
S	Belgium	
B	Italy	

KEIRIN

G	Florian Rousseau	FRA
S	Gary Neiwand	AUS
B	Jens Fiedler	GER

MOUNTAIN BIKE

G	Miguel Martinez	FRA
S	Filip Meirhaeghe	BEL
B	Christoph Sauser	SUI
7	Cadel Evans	AUS
10	Paul Rowney	AUS
13	Rob Woods	AUS

WOMEN

ROAD RACE

G	Leontien Zijlaard	NED
S	Hanka Kupfernagel	GER
B	Diana Ziliute	LTU
4	Anna Wilson	AUS
23	Tracey Gaudry	AUS
28	Juanita Feldhahn	AUS

INDIVIDUAL TIME TRIAL (ROAD)

G	Leontien Zijlaard	NED
S	Mari Holden	USA
B	Jeannie Longo-Ciprelli	FRA
4	Anna Wilson	AUS
21	Tracey Gaudry	AUS

500M TIME TRIAL (TRACK)

G	Felicia Ballanger	FRA
S	Michelle Ferris	AUS
B	Cuihua Jiang	CHN
14	Lyndelle Higginson	AUS

3000M INDIVIDUAL PURSUIT

G	Leontien Zijlaard	NED
S	Marion Clignet	FRA
B	Yvonne McGregor	GBR
7	Alayna Burns	AUS

SPRINT

G	Felicia Ballanger	FRA
S	Oxana Grichina	RUS
B	Iryna Yanovych	UKR
4	Michelle Ferris	AUS

POINTS RACE

G	Antonella Bellutti	ITA
S	Leontien Zijlaard	NED
B	Olga Slioussareva	RUS
9	Alayna Burns	AUS

MOUNTAIN BIKE

G	Paola Pezzo	ITA
S	Barbara Blatter	SUI
B	Margarita Fullana	ESP
6	Mary Grigson	AUS
21	Anna Baylis	AUS

DIVING

MEN

3M SPRINGBOARD

G	Xiong Ni	CHN
S	Fernando Platas	MEX
B	Dmitri Saoutine	RUS
5	Dean Pullar	AUS
15	Robert Newbery	AUS

10M PLATFORM

G	Liang Tian	CHN
S	Jia Hu	CHN
B	Dmitri Saoutine	RUS
8	Matthew Helm	AUS
10	Robert Newbery	AUS

SYNCHRONISED SPRINGBOARD

G	China	
S	Russian Federation	
B	Australia Robert Newbery/Dean Pullar	

SYNCHRONISED PLATFORM

G	Russian Federation	
S	China	
B	Germany	
5	Australia Matthew Helm/Robert Newbery	

WOMEN

3M SPRINGBOARD

G	Mingxia Fu	CHN
S	Jinging Guo	CHN
B	Doerte Linder	GER
7	Chantelle Michell	AUS
SF	Rebecca Gilmore	AUS

10M PLATFORM

G	Laura Wilkinson	USA
S	Na Li	CHN
B	Anne Montminy	CAN
11	Rebecca Gilmore	AUS
24	Loudy Tourky	AUS

SYNCHRONISED SPRINGBOARD

G	Russian Federation	
S	China	
B	Ukraine	
4	Australia Chantelle Michell/Loudy Tourky	

SYNCHRONIZED PLATFORM

G	China	
S	Canada	
B	Australia Loudy Tourky/Rebecca Gilmore	

EQUESTRIAN

INDIVIDUAL THREE-DAY EVENT

G	David O'Connor	USA
S	Andrew Hoy	AUS
B	Mark Todd	NZL
16	Brook Staples	AUS
20	Amanda Ross	AUS

TEAM THREE-DAY EVENT

G	Australia - Andrew Hoy, Phillip Dutton, Matt Ryan, Stuart Tinney	
S	Great Britain	
B	United States	

INDIVIDUAL DRESSAGE

G	Anky van Grunsven	NED
S	Isabell Werth	GER
B	Ulla Salzgeber	GER
9	Kristy Oatley-Nist	AUS
33	Rachael Downs	AUS
34	Mary Hanna	AUS
35	Ricky Macmillan	AUS

TEAM DRESSAGE

G	Germany	
S	Netherlands	
B	United States	
6	Australia - Rachael Downs, Mary Hanna, Kristy Oatley-Nist, Ricky MacMillan	

INDIVIDUAL JUMPING

G	Jeroen Dubbeldam	NED
S	Albert Voorn	NED
B	Khaled Al Eid	KSA
20	Geoff Bloomfield	AUS
43	Jamie Coman	AUS
DNQ	Gavin Chester	AUS
DNQ	Ron Easey	AUS

TEAM JUMPING

G	Germany	
S	Switzerland	
B	Brazil	
10	Australia - Gavin Chester, Jamie Coman, Ron Easey, Geoff Bloomfield	

FENCING

MEN

INDIVIDUAL ÉPÉE

G	Pavel Kolobkov	RUS
S	Hugues Obry	FRA
B	Sang-Ki Lee	KOR
15	Gerard Adams	AUS
39	Nick Heffernan	AUS
41	David Nathan	AUS

TEAM ÉPÉE

G	Italy	
S	France	
B	Cuba	
8	Australia – Luc Cartillier, Gerard Adams, Nick Heffernan	

INDIVIDUAL FOIL

G	Kim Young-Ho	KOR
S	Ralf Bissdorf	GER

B Dmitri Chevtchenko   RUS

R1 Gerald McMahon   AUS

TEAM FOIL

G France

S China

B Italy

INDIVIDUAL SABRE

G Mihai Claudiu Covaliu   ROM

S Mathieu Gourdain   FRA

B Wiradech Kothny   GER

TEAM SABRE

G Russian Federation

S France

B Germany

WOMEN

INDIVIDUAL ÉPÉE

G Timea Nagy   HUN

S Gianna Habluetzel-Buerki   SUI

B Laura Flessel-Colovic   FRA

R2 Evelyn Halls   AUS

TEAM ÉPÉE

G Russian Federation

S Switzerland

B China

INDIVIDUAL FOIL

G Valentina Vezzali   ITA

S Rita Koenig   GER

B Biovanna Trillini   ITA

R1 Jo Halls   AUS

TEAM FOIL

G Italy

S Poland

B Germany

FOOTBALL

MEN

G Cameroon

S Spain

B Chile

Australia — Con Blatsis, Marco Bresciano, Simon Colosimo, Jason Culina, Michael Curcija, Joey Didulica, Brett Emerton, Hayden Foxe, Vince Grella, Stephen Laybutt, Stan Lazaridis, Danny Milosevic, Lucas Neill, Nick Rizzo, Josip Skoko, Mark Viduka, Kasey Wehrman, Clayton Zane

WOMEN

G Norway

S United States

B Germany

Australia — Dianne Alagich, Sharon Black, Bryony Duus, Alicia Ferguson, Alison Forman, Heather Garriock, Kelly Golebiowski, Peita-Claire Hepperlin, Sunni Hughes, Kate McShea, Julie Murray, Cheryl Salisbury, Bridgette Starr, Anissa Tann-Darby, Leanne Trimboli, Sacha Wainwright, Tracey Wheeler, Amy Wilson

GYMNASTICS-ARTISTIC

MEN

TEAM

G China

S Ukraine

B Russian Federation

INDIVIDUAL ALL-AROUND

G Alexei Nemov   RUS

S Wei Yang   CHN

B Oleksandr Beresh   UKR

29 Phillipe Rizzo   AUS

DNQ Damian Istria   AUS

FLOOR EXERCISE

G Igors Vihrovs   LAT

S Alexei Nemov   RUS

B Iordan Iovtchev   BUL

DNQ Damian Istria   AUS

DNQ Phillipe Rizzo   AUS

POMMEL HORSE

G Marius Urzica   ROM

S Eric Poujade   FRA

B Alexei Nemov   RUS

DNQ Damian Istria   AUS

DNQ Phillipe Rizzo   AUS

RINGS

G Szilveszter Csollany   HUN

S Dimosathenis Tampakos   GRE

B Iordan Iovtchev   BUL

VAULT

G Gervasio Deferr   ESP

S Alexey Bondarenko   RUS

B Leszek Blanik   POL

DNQ Damian Istria   AUS

DNQ Phillipe Rizzo   AUS

PARALLEL BARS

G Xiaopeng Li   CHN

S Joo-Hyung Lee   KOR

B Alexei Nemov   RUS

DNQ Damian Istria   AUS

DNQ Phillipe Rizzo   AUS

HORIZONTAL BAR

G Alexei Nemov   RUS

S Benjamin Varonian   FRA

B Joo-Hyung Lee   KOR

WOMEN

TEAM

G Romania

S Russian Federation

B China

7 Australia - Melinda Cleland, Alexandra Croak, Trudy McIntosh, Lisa Skinner, Allana Slater, Brooke Walker

---

INDIVIDUAL ALL-AROUND

G Simona Amanar   ROM

S Maria Olaru   ROM

B Xuan Liu   CHN

8 Lisa Skinner   AUS

16 Allana Slater   AUS

38 Brooke Walker   AUS

52 Trudy McIntosh   AUS

56 Alexander Croak   AUS

65 Melinda Cleland   AUS

VAULT

G Elena Zamolodtchikova   RUS

S Andreea Raducan   ROM

B Ekaterina Lobazniouk   RUS

DNQ Melinda Cleland   AUS

DNQ Trudy McIntosh   AUS

DNQ Lisa Skinner   AUS

DNQ Allana Slater   AUS

DNQ Brooke Walker   AUS

UNEVEN BARS

G Svetlana Khorkina   RUS

S Jie Ling   CHN

B Yun Yang   CHN

DNQ Alexandra Cook   AUS

DNQ Melinda Cleland   AUS

DNQ Lisa Skinner   AUS

DNQ Allana Slater   AUS

DNQ Brooke Walker   AUS

BALANCE BEAM

G Xuan Liu   CHN

S Ekaterina Lobazniouk   RUS

B Elena Prodounova   RUS

DNQ Alexandra Cook   AUS

DNQ Trudy McIntosh   AUS

DNQ Lisa Skinner   AUS

DNQ Allana Slater   AUS

DNQ Brooke Walker   AUS

FLOOR EXERCISE

G Elena Zamolodtchikova   RUS

S Svetlana Khorkina   RUS

B Simona Amanar   ROM

8 Lisa Skinner   AUS

DNQ Alexandra Cook   AUS

DNQ Trudy McIntosh   AUS

DNQ Allana Slater   AUS

DNQ Brooke Walker   AUS

GYMNASTICS-RHYTHMIC

INDIVIDUAL ALL-AROUND

G Yulia Barsukova   RUS

S Yulia Raskina   BLR

B Alina Kabaeva   RUS

19 Dani Leray   AUS

GROUP ALL-AROUND

G Russian Federation

S Belarus

B Greece

GYMNASTICS-TRAMPOLINE

MEN

G Alexandre Moskalenko   RUS

S Ji Wallace   AUS

B Mathieu Turgeon   CAN

WOMEN

G Irina Karavaeva   RUS

S Oxana Tsyhuleva   UKR

B Karen Cockburn   CAN

10 Robyn Forbes   AUS

HANDBALL

MEN

G Russian Federation

S Sweden

B Spain

12 Australia - Peter Bach, Cristian Bajan, Vernon Cheung, Russell Garnett, David Gonzalez, Kristian Groenintwoud, Daryl McCormack, Rajan Pavlovic, Taip Ramadami, Lee Schofield, Dragan Sestic, Sasa Sestic, Karim Shehab, Milan Slavujevic, Brendon Taylor

WOMEN

G Denmark

S Hungary

B Norway

10 Australia – Janni Bach, Petra Besta, Rina Bjarnason, Raelene Boulton, Kim Briggs, Mari Edland, Sarah Hammond, Fiona Hannan, Vera Ignjatovic, Jana Jamnicky, Lydia Kahmke, Marina Kopcalic, Jovana Milosevic, Shelley Ormes, Katrina Shinfield

HOCKEY

MEN

G Netherlands

S South Korea

B Australia – Michael Brennan, Adam Commens, Stephen Davies, Daom Diletti, Lachlan Dreher, Jason Duff, Troy Elder, James Elmer, Paul Gaudoin, Stephen Hold, Brent Livermore, Daniel Sproule, Jay Stacey, Craig Victory, Matthew Wells, Michael York

WOMEN

G Australia – Kate Allen, Lisa Carruthers, Renita Garard, Alyson Annan, Juliet Haslam, Rechelle Hawkes, Nikki Hudson, Rachel Imison, Clover Maitland, Claire Mitchell-Taverner, Jenny Morris, Alison Peek, Katrina Powell, Angie Skirving, Kate Starre, Julie Towers

S Argentina

B Netherlands

JUDO

MEN

60KG

G Tadihiro Nomura   JPN

S	Bu-Kyung Jung	KOR
B	Manolo Poulot	CUB
B	Aidyn Smagulov	KGZ
R2	Adrian Robertson	AUS

66KG

G	Huseyin Ozkan	TUR
S	Larbi Benboudaoud	FRA
B	Girolamo Giovinazzo	ITL
B	Giorgi Vazagashvili	GEO
R3	Andrew Collett	AUS

73KG

G	Guiseppe Maddaloni	ITA
S	Tiago Camilo	BRA
B	Vsevolods Zelonijs	LAT
B	Anatoly Laryukov	BLR
R2	Tom Hill	AUS

81KG

G	Makoto Takimoto	JPN
S	In-Chul Cho	KOR
B	Nuno Delgado	POR
B	Aleksei Budolin	EST
9	Daniel Kelly	AUS

90KG

G	Mark Huizing	NED
S	Carlos Honorato	BRA
B	Frederic Demont	FRA
B	Rusian Mashurenko	UKR
R5	Robert Ivers	AUS

100KG

G	Kosei Inoue	JPN
S	Nicolas Gill	CAN
B	Iouri Stepkine	RUS
B	Stephane Traineau	FRA
R2	Daniel Rusitovic	AUS

100+ KG

G	David Douillet	FRA
S	Shinichi Shinohara	JPN
B	Indrek Pertelson	EST
B	Tamerlan Tmenov	RUS
R2	Robert Ball	AUS

WOMEN

48KG

G	Ryoko Tanura	JPN
S	Lioubov Brouletova	RUS
B	Anna-Maria Gradante	GER
B	Ann Simons	BEL
R2	Jenny Hill	AUS

52KG

G	Legna Verdecia	CUB
S	Noriko Narazaki	JPN
B	Sun Hui Kye	PRK
B	Yuxiang Liu	CHN
9	Rebecca Sullivan	AUS

57KG

G	Isabel Fernandez	ESP
S	Driulys Gonzalez	CUB
B	Maria Pekli	AUS
B	Kie Kusakabe	JPN

63KG

G	Severine Vandenhende	FRA
S	Shufang Li	CHN
B	Sung-Sook Jung	KOR
B	Gella Vandecaveye	BEL
R1	Carly Dixon	AUS

70KG

G	Sibells Veranes	CUB
S	Kate Howey	GBR
B	Ylenia Scapin	ITA
B	Min-Sun Cho	KOR
R4	Cath Arlove	AUS

78KG

G	Lin Tang	CHN
S	Celine Lebrun	FRA
B	Simona Richter	ROM
B	Emanuela Pierantozzi	ITA
R2	Natalie Jenkinson	AUS

78+ KG

G	Hua Yuan	CHN
S	Daima Mayelis Beltran	CUB
B	Seon-Young Kim	KOR

B	Mayumi Yamashita	JPN
R2	Caroline Curren	AUS

MODERN PENTATHLON

MEN

G	Dmitry Svatkovsky	RUS
S	Gabor Balogh	HUN
B	Pavel Dovgal	BLR
20	Robert McGregor	AUS

WOMEN

G	Stephanie Cook	GBR
S	Emily de Riel	USA
B	Kate Allenby	GBR
14	Kitty Chiller	AUS

ROWING

MEN

SINGLE SCULLS

G	Rob Waddell	NZL
S	Xeno Mueller	SUI
B	Marcel Hacker	GER

DOUBLE SCULLS

G Slovenia

S Norway

B Italy

LIGHTWEIGHT DOUBLE SCULLS

G Poland

S Italy

B France

7 Australia - Haimish Karrasch, Bruce Hick

QUADRUPLE SCULLS

G Italy

S Netherlands

B Germany

4 Australia - Peter Hardcastle, Jason Day, Stuart Reside, Duncan Free

PAIRS WITHOUT COX

G France

S United States

B Australia - Matthew Long, James Tomkins

FOURS WITHOUT COX

G Great Britain

S Italy

B Australia - James Stewart, Ben Dodwell, Geoff Stewart, Bo Hanson

LIGHTWEIGHT FOURS WITHOUT COX

G France

S Australia - Simon Burgess, Anthony Edwards, Darren Balmforth, Robert Richards

B Denmark

EIGHTS

G Great Britain

S Australia - Daniel Burke, Alastair Gordon, Brett Hayman, Nick Porzig, Christian Ryan, Stuart Welch, Jaime Fernandez, Mike McKay, Robert Jahrling

B Croatia

WOMEN

SINGLE SCULLS

G	Ekaterina Karsten	BLR
S	Rumyana Neykova	BUL
B	Katrin Rutschow	GER
5	Georgina Douglas	AUS

DOUBLE SCULLS

G Germany

S Netherlands

B Lithuania

6 Australia - Marina Katzakis, Bronwyn Roye

LIGHTWEIGHT DOUBLE SCULLS

G Romania

S Germany

B United States

4 Australia - Sally Newmarch, Virginia Lee

QUADRUPLE SCULLS

G Germany

S Great Britain

B Russian Federation

7 Australia - Kerry Knowler, Monique Heinke, Julia Wilson, Sally Robbins

PAIRS WITHOUT COX

G Romania

S Australia - Rachael Taylor, Kate Slatter

B USA

EIGHTS

G Romania

S Netherlands

B Canada

5 Australia - Victoria Roberts, Alison Davies, Jodi Winter, Bronwyn Thompson, Rachael Kininmonth, Kristina Larsen, Emily Martin, Jane Robinson, Katie Foulkes

SAILING

MEN

470

G Australia - Tom King, Mark Turnbull

S United States

B Argentina

FINN

G Iain Percy — GBR

S Luca Devoti — ITA

B Fredrik Loof — SWE

13 Anthony Nossiter — AUS

MISTRAL

G Christoph Sieber — AUT

S Carlos Espinola — ARG

B Aaron McIntosh — NZL

4 Lars Kleppich — AUS

49ER

G Finland

S Great Britain

B United States

6 Australia - Chris Nicholson, Daniel Phillips

LASER

G Ben Ainslie — GBR

S Robert Scheidt — BRA

B Michael Blackburn — AUS

SOLING

G Denmark

S Germany

B Norway

8 Australia – David Edwards, Josh Grace, Neville Wittey

STAR

G United States

S Great Britain

B Brazil

7 Australia - Colin Beashel, David Giles

TORNADO

G Austria

S Australia - Darren Bundock, John Forbes

B Germany

WOMEN

470

G Australia - Jenny Armstrong, Belinda Stowell

S United States

B Ukraine

EUROPE

G Shirley Robertson — GBR

S Margaret Matthysse — NED

B Serena Amato — ARG

15 Melanie Dennison — AUS

MISTRAL

G Alessandra Sensini — ITA

S Amelie Lux — GER

B Barbara Kendall — NZL

5 Jessica Crisp — AUS

SHOOTING

MEN

10M AIR PISTOL

G Frank Dumoulin — FRA

S Yifu Wang — CHN

B Igor Basinksy — BLR

32 David Moore — AUS

38 David Porter — AUS

25M RAPID-FIRE PISTOL

G Serguei Alifirenko — RUS

S Michel Ansermet — SUI

B Iulian Raicea — ROM

20 David Chapman — AUS

50M PISTOL

G Tanyu Kiriakov — BUL

S Igor Basinsky — BLR

B Martin Tenk — CZE

18 David Moore — AUS

20 David Porter — AUS

10M RUNNING TARGET

G Yang Ling — CHN

S Oleg Moldovan — MDA

B Zhiyuan Niu — CHN

12 David Jones — AUS

17 Adam Gitsham — AUS

10M AIR RIFLE

G Yalin Cai — CHN

S Artem Khadjibekov — RUS

B Evgueni Aleinikov — RUS

---

27 Timothy Lowndes — AUS

41 Robert Wieland — AUS

50M RIFLE, 3-POSITION

G Rajmond Debevec — SLO

S Juha Hirvi — FIN

B Harald Stenvaag — NOR

20 Timothy Lowndes — AUS

22 Samuel Wieland — AUS

50M RIFLE, PRONE POSITION

G Jonas Edman — SWE

S Torben Grimmel — DEN

B Sergei Martynov — BLR

19 Timothy Lowndes — AUS

19 Warren Potent — AUS

TRAP

G Michael Diamond — AUS

S Ian Peel — GBR

B Giovanni Pellielo — ITA

13 Russell Mark — AUS

DOUBLE TRAP

G Richard Faulds — GBR

S Russell Mark — AUS

B Fehaid Al Deehani — KUW

9 Michael Diamond — AUS

SKEET

G Mykola Mikcheve — UKR

S Patr Malek — CZE

B James Graves — USA

14 Clive Barton — AUS

39 David Cunningham — AUS

WOMEN

10M AIR PISTOL

G Luna Tao — CHN

S Jasna Sekaric — YUG

B Annemarie Forder — AUS

28 Linda Ryan — AUS

25M PISTOL

G Maria Grozdeva — BUL

S Luna Tao — CHN

B Lolita Evglevskaya — BLR

11 Linda Ryan — AUS

15 Christine Trefry — AUS

10M AIR RIFLE

G Nancy Johnson — USA

S Cho-Hyun Kang — KOR

B Jing Gao — CHN

15 Sue McCready — AUS

41 Belinda Imgrund — AUS

50M RIFLE, 3-POSITION

G Renata Mauer-Rozanska — POL

S Tatiana Goldobina — RUS

B Maria Feklistova — RUS

20 Sue McCready — AUS

39 Carrie Quigley — AUS

TRAP

G Daina Gudzineviciute — LTU

S Delphine Racinet — FRA

B E Gao — CHN

10 Lisa Smith — AUS

12 Deserie Wakefield-Baynes — AUS

DOUBLE TRAP

G Pia Hansen — SWE

S Deborah Gelisio — ITA

B Kimberly Rhode — USA

9 Ann Maree Roberts — AUS

12 Deserie Wakefield-Baynes — AUS

SKEET

G Zemfira Meftakhetdinova — AZE

S Svetlana Demina — RUS

B Diana Igaly — HUN

4 Tash Lonsdale — AUS

SOFTBALL

WOMEN

G United States

S Japan

B Australia - Sandra Allen, Joanne Brown, Kerry Dienelt, Peta Edebone, Sue Fairhurst,

Selina Follas, Fiona Hanes, Kelly Hardie, Tanya Harding, Sally McCreedy, Simmone Morrow, Melanie Roche, Natalie Titcume, Natalie Ward, Brooke Wilkins

SWIMMING

MEN

50M FREESTYLE
G	Anthony Ervin	USA
G	Gary Hall Jr	USA
B	Pieter van den Hoogenband	NED
DNQ	Brett Hawke	AUS
DNQ	Chris Fydler	AUS

100M FREESTYLE
G	Pieter van den Hoogenband	NED
S	Alexander Popov	RUS
B	Gary Hall Jr	USA
4	Michael Klim	AUS
8	Chris Fydler	AUS

200M FREESTYLE
G	Pieter van den Hoogenband	NED
S	Ian Thorpe	AUS
B	Massimiliano Rosolino	ITA
8	Grant Hackett	AUS

400M FREESTYLE
G	Ian Thorpe	AUS
S	Massimiliano Rosolino	ITA
B	Klete Keller	USA
7	Grant Hackett	AUS

1500M FREESTYLE
G	Grant Hackett	AUS
S	Kieren Perkins	AUS
B	Chris Thompson	USA

100M BACKSTROKE
G	Lenny Krayzelburg	USA
S	Matthew Welsh	AUS
B	Stev Theloke	GER
4	Josh Watson	AUS

200M BACKSTROKE
G	Lenny Krayzelburg	USA
S	Aaron Peirsol	USA
B	Matthew Welsh	AUS
DNQ	Cameron Delaney	AUS

100M BREASTSTROKE
G	Domenico Fioravanti	ITA
S	Ed Moses	USA
B	Roman Sloudnov	RUS
DNQ	Phil Rogers	AUS

200M BREASTSTROKE
G	Domenico Fioravanti	ITA
S	Terrence Parkin	RSA
B	Davide Rummolo	ITA
4	Regan Harrison	AUS
8	Ryan Mitchell	AUS

100M BUTTERFLY
G	Lars Froelander	SWE
S	Michael Klim	AUS
B	Geoff Huegill	AUS

200M BUTTERFLY
G	Tom Malchow	USA
S	Denys Sylant'yev	UKR
B	Justin Norris	AUS
DNQ	Heath Ramsey	AUS

200M INDIVIDUAL MEDLEY
G	Massimiliano Rosolino	ITA
S	Tom Dolan	USA
B	Tom Wilkens	USA
DNQ	Matthew Dunn	AUS
DNQ	Robert van der Zant	AUS

400M INDIVIDUAL MEDLEY
G	Tom Dolan	USA
S	Erik Vendt	USA
B	Curtis Myden	CAN
6	Justin Norris	AUS
DNQ	Matthew Dunn	AUS

4X100M FREESTYLE RELAY
G	Australia – Michael Klim, Chris Fydler, Ashley Callus, Ian Thorpe, (Todd Pearson, Adam Pine)	
S	United States	
B	Brazil	

4X200M FREESTYLE RELAY
G	Australia – Ian Thorpe, Michael Klim, Todd Pearson, William Kirby, (Daniel Kowalski, Grant Hackett)	
S	United States	
B	Netherlands	

4X100M MEDLEY RELAY
G	United States	
S	Australia – Matthew Welsh, Regan Harrison, Geoff Huegill, Michael Klim, (Josh Watson, Ryan Mitchell, Adam Pine, Ian Thorpe)	
B	Germany	

WOMEN

50M FREESTYLE
G	Inge de Bruijn	NED
S	Therese Alshammar	SWE
B	Dara Torres	USA
DNQ	Susie O'Neill	AUS
DNQ	Sarah Ryan	AUS

100M FREESTYLE
G	Inge de Bruijn	NED
S	Therese Alshammar	SWE
B	Dara Torres	USA
B	Jenny Thompson	USA
DNQ	Sarah Ryan	AUS
DNQ	Susie O'Neill	AUS

200M FREESTYLE
G	Susie O'Neill	AUS
S	Martina Moravcova	SVK
B	Claudia Poll	CRC
DNQ	Giann Rooney	AUS

400M FREESTYLE
G	Brooke Bennett	USA
S	Diana Munz	USA
B	Claudia Poll	CRC
DNQ	Kasey Giteau	AUS
DNQ	Sarah D'Arcy	AUS

800M FREESTYLE
G	Brooke Bennett	USA
S	Yana Klochkova	RUS
B	Kaitlin Sandeno	USA
DNQ	Hayley Lewis	AUS
DNQ	Rachel Harris	AUS

100M BACKSTROKE
G	Diana Mocanu	ROM
S	Mai Nakamura	JPN
B	Nina Zhivanevskaya	ESP
7	Dyana Calub	AUS

200M BACKSTROKE
G	Diana Mocanu	ROM
S	Roxana Maracineanu	FRA
B	Miki Nakao	JPN
DNQ	Clementine Stoney	AUS
DNQ	Dyana Calub	AUS

100M BREASTSTROKE
G	Megan Quann	USA
S	Leisel Jones	AUS
B	Penny Heyns	RSA
7	Tarnee White	AUS

200M BREASTSTROKE
G	Agnes Kovacs	HUN
S	Kristy Kowal	USA
B	Amanda Beard	USA
DNQ	Rebecca Brown	AUS
DNQ	Caroline Hildreth	AUS

100M BUTTERFLY
G	Inge de Bruijn	NED
S	Martina Moravcova	SVK
B	Dara Torres	USA
4	Petria Thomas	AUS
7	Susie O'Neill	AUS

200M BUTTERFLY
G	Misty Hyman	USA
S	Susie O'Neill	AUS
B	Petria Thomas	AUS

200M INDIVIDUAL MEDLEY
G	Yana Klochkova	UKR
S	Beatrice Caslaru	ROM
B	Cristina Teuscher	USA
DNQ	Elli Overton	AUS
DNQ	Anna Windsor	AUS

400M INDIVIDUAL MEDLEY
G	Yana Klochkova	UKR
S	Yasuko Tajima	JPN
B	Beatrice Caslaru	ROM
8	Jennifer Reilly	AUS
DNQ	Rachel Harris	AUS

4X100M FREESTYLE RELAY
G	United States	
S	Netherlands	
B	Sweden	
6	Australia - Susie O'Neill, Sarah Ryan, Elka Graham, Giaan Rooney, (Mel Dodd)	

4X200M FREESTYLE RELAY
G	United States	
S	Australia - Susie O'Neill, Giaan Rooney, Kirsten Thomson, Petria Thomas, (Elka Graham, Jacinta van Lint)	
B	Germany	

4X100M MEDLEY RELAY
G	United States	
S	Australia – Dyana Calub, Leisel Jones, Petria Thomas, Susie O'Neill, (Giaan Rooney, Tarnee White, Sarah Ryan)	
B	Japan	

SYNCHRONISED SWIMMING

DUET

- G Russian Federation
- S Japan
- B France
- 16 Australia - Irena Olevsky, Naomi Young

TEAM

- G Russian Federation
- S Japan
- B Canada
- 8 Australia - Tracey Davis, Kelly Geraghty, Amanda Laird, Dannielle Liesch, Katrina Orpwood, Rachel Ren, Cathryn Wightman, Naomi Young, Irena Olevsky

TABLE TENNIS

MEN

SINGLES

G	Linghui Kong	CHN
S	Jan-Ove Waldner	SWE
B	Guoliang Liu	CHN
DNQ	Simon Gerada	AUS
DNQ	Russ Lavale	AUS
DNQ	Mark Smythe	AUS

DOUBLES

G	Liqin Wang/Sen Yan	CHN
S	Linghui Kong/Guoliang Liu	CHN
B	Chila/Gatien	FRA
DNQ	Australia - Brett Clarke/ Jeff Plumb, Simon Gerada/ Mark Smythe	

WOMEN

SINGLES

G	Nan Wang	CHN
S	Ju Li	CHN
B	Jing Chen	TPE
DNQ	Miao Miao	AUS
DNQ	Stella Zhou	AUS
DNQ	Shirley Zhou	AUS

DOUBLES

G	Ju Li/Nan Wang	CHN
S	Jin Sun/Ying Yang	CHN
B	Kim/Ryu	KOR
QF	Miao Miao/Shirley Zhou	AUS
DNQ	Jian Fang Lay/Stella Zhou	AUS

TAEKWONDO

MEN

58KG

G	Michail Mouroutsos	GRE
S	Gabriel Esparza	ESP
B	Chih-Hsiung Huang	TPE
R1	Paul Lyons	AUS

68KG

G	Steven Lopez	USA
S	Joon-Sik Sin	KOR
B	Hadi Saeibonehkohal	IRI
REP	Carlo Massimino	AUS

80KG

G	Angel Fuentes	CUB
S	Faissal Ebnoutalib	GER
B	Victor Garibay	MEX
REP	Warren Hansen	AUS

80+KG

G	Kyong-Hun Kim	KOR
S	Daniel Trenton	AUS
B	Pascal Gentil	FRA

WOMEN

49KG

G	Lauren Burns	AUS
S	Urbia MelendezRodriguez	CUB
B	Shu-Ju Chi	TPE

57KG

G	Jae-Eun Jung	KOR
S	Hieu Ngan Tran	VIE
B	Hamide Bikcin	TUR
R1	Cynthia Cameron	AUS

67KG

G	Sun-Hee Lee	KOR
S	Trude Gundersen	NOR
B	Yoriko Okamoto	JPN
R1	Lisa O'Keefe	AUS

67+KG

G	Zhong Chen	CHN
S	Natalia Ivanova	RUS
B	Dominique Bosshart	CAN
REP	Tanya White	AUS

TENNIS

MEN

SINGLES

G	Yevgeny Kafelnikov	RUS
S	Tommy Haas	GER
B	Arnaud Di Pasquale	FRA
R1	Lleyton Hewitt	AUS
R1	Andrew Ilie	AUS
R3	Mark Philippoussis	AUS
R2	Pat Rafter	AUS

DOUBLES

G	Canada	
S	Australia - Mark Woodforde/ Todd Woodbridge	
B	Spain	

WOMEN

SINGLES

G	Venus Williams	USA
S	Elena Dementieva	RUS
B	Monica Seles	USA
SF	Jelena Dokic	AUS
R1	Alicia Molik	AUS
R2	Nicole Pratt	AUS

DOUBLES

G	United States	
S	Netherlands	
B	Belgium	
R2	Australia - Jelena Dokic/ Rennae Stubbs	

TRIATHLON

MEN

G	Simon Whitfield	CAN
S	Stephen Vuckovic	GER
B	Jan Rehula	CZE
6	Miles Stewart	AUS
27	Craig Walton	AUS
34	Peter Robertson	AUS

WOMEN

G	Brigitte McMahon	SUI
S	Michellie Jones	AUS
B	Magali Messmer	SUI
5	Loretta Harrop	AUS
9	Nicole Hackett	AUS

VOLLEYBALL-INDOOR

MEN

- G Yugoslavia
- S Russian Federation
- B Italy
- 8 Australia – Daniel Howard, Steve Keir, Benjamin Hardy, Nathan Jakavicius, Russell Wentworth, Daniel Ronan, Spiros Marazios, Scott Newcomb, David Beard, Benjamin Loft, Hidde van Beest, Mark Williams

WOMEN

- G Cuba
- S Russian Federation
- B Brazil
- 9 Australia - Liz Brett, Tamsin Barnett, Louise Bawden, Majella Brown, Angela Clarke, Bea Daly, Renae Maycock, Christie Mokotupu, Sil Ruddle, Selina Scoble, Sandi Bowen, Rachel White

VOLLEYBALL-BEACH

MEN

- G United States
- S Brazil
- B Germany
- Australia
- R4 Lee Zahner/Julien Prosser
- R3 Matt Grinlaubs/Joshua Slack

WOMEN

- G Australia - Natalie Cook/ Kerri Pottharst
- S Brazil
- B Brazil
- Australia
- QF Tania Gooley/Pauline Manser
- R1 Annette Huygens-Tholen/ Sarah Stratton

WATERPOLO

MEN

- G Hungary
- S Russian Federation
- B Yugoslavia
- 8 Australia – Sean Boyd, Eddie Denis, Andrei Kovalenko, Daniel Marsden, Craig Miller, Timothy Neesham, Mark Oberman, Rod Owen-Jones, Rafael Sterk, Nathan Thomas, Grant Waterman, Thomas Whalan, Gavin Woods

WOMEN

- G Australia - Naomi Castle, Joanne Fox, Bridgette Gusterson, Simone Hankin, Yvette Higgins, Kate Hooper, Bronwyn Maher, Gail Miller, Melissa Mills, Debbie Watson, Liz Weekes, Danielle Woodhouse, Taryn Woods
- S United States
- B Russian Federation

WEIGHTLIFTING

MEN

56KG

G	Halil Mutlu	TUR
S	Wenxiong Wu	CHN
B	Xiangxiang Zhang	CHN
17	Mehmet Yagci	AUS

62KG

G	Nikolay Pechalov	CRO
S	Leonidas Sabanis	GRE
B	Gennady Oleshchuk	BLR
9	Yurik Sarkisian	AUS

69KG

G	Galabin Boveski	BUL
S	Georgi Markov	BUL
B	Sergei Lavrenov	BLR

77KG

G	Xugang Zhan	CHN
S	Viktor Mitrou	GRE
B	Arsen Melikyan	ARM
14	Damien Brown	AUS

85KG

G	Pyrros Dimas	GRE
S	Marc Huster	GER
B	George Asanidze	GEO
6	Sergo Chakhoyan	AUS

94KG

G	Akakios Kakiasvilis	GRE
S	Szymon Kolecki	POL
B	Alexei Petrov	RUS
10	Aleksan Karapetyan	AUS
14	Kiril Kounev	AUS

105KG

G	Hossein Tavakoli	IRI
S	Alan Tsagaev	BUL
B	Said S Asaad	QAT

105+KG

G	Hossein Rezazadeh	IRI
S	Ronny Weller	GER
B	Andrei Chemerkin	RUS
18	Anthony Martin	AUS
19	Chris Rae	AUS

WOMEN

48KG

G	Tara Nott	USA
S	Raema Lisa Rumbewas	INA
B	Sri Indriyani	INA

53KG

G	Xia Yang	CHN
S	Feng-Ying Li	TPE
B	Winarni Binti Slamet	INA

58KG

G	Soraya Jimenez Mendivil	MEX
S	Song Hui Ri	PRK
B	Khassaraporn Suta	THA
10	Natasha Barker	AUS
12	Meagan Warthold	AUS

63KG

G	Xiaomin Chen	CHN
S	Valentina Popova	RUS
B	Ioanna Chatziioannou	GRE
6	Amanda Phillips	AUS

69KG

G	Weining Lin	CHN
S	Erzsebet Markus	HUN
B	Karnam Malleswari	IND
9	Michelle Kettner	AUS

75KG

G	Maria Isabel Urrutia	COL
S	Ruth Ogbeifo	NGR
B	Yi-Hang Kuo	TPE

75+KG

G	Meiyuan Ding	CHN
S	Agata Wrobei	POL
B	Cheryl Haworth	USA

WRESTLING-FREESTYLE

54KG

G	Namig Abdullayev	AZE
S	Samuel Henson	USA
B	Amiran Karntanov	GRE

58KG

G	Alireza Dabir	IRI
S	Yevgen Buslovych	UKR
B	Terry Brands	USA
R1	Cory O'Brien	AUS

63KG

G	Mourad Oumakhanov	RUS
S	Serafim Barzakov	BUL
B	Jae Sung Jang	KOR
R1	Musa Ilhan	AUS

69KG

G	Daniel Igali	CAN
S	Arsen Gitinov	RUS
B	Lincoln McIlravy	USA
R1	Cameron Johnston	AUS

76KG

G	Alexander Leipold	GER
S	Brandon Slay	USA
B	Eui Jae Moon	KOR
R1	Rein Ozoline	AUS

85KG

G	Adam Saitiev	RUS
S	Yoel Romero	CUB
B	Mogamed Ibragimov	MKD
R1	Igor Praporshchikov	AUS

97KG

G	Saghid Mourtasaliyev	RUS
S	Islam Bairamukov	KAZ
B	Eldar Kurtanidze	GEO
R1	Gabriel Szerda	AUS

130KG

G	David Moussoulbes	RUS
S	Artur Taymazov	UZB
B	Alexis Rodriguez	CUB
DNC	Mushtaq Abdullah	AUS

WRESTLING-GRECO-ROMAN

54KG

G	Kwon Ho Sim	KOR
S	Lazaro Rivas	CUB
B	Yong Gyun Kang	PRK

58KG

G	Armen Nazarian	BUL
S	In-Sub Kim	KOR
B	Zetian Sheng	CHN
R1	Brett Cash	AUS

63KG

G	Varteres Samourgachev	RUS
S	Juan Luis Maren	CUB
B	Akaki Chachua	GEO

69KG

G	Filiberto Azcuy	CUB
S	Katsuhiko Nagata	JPN
B	Alexei Glouchkov	RUS
20	Ali Abdo	AUS

76KG

G	Mourat Kardanov	RUS
S	Matt James Lindland	USA
B	Marko Yil-Hannuksela	FIN

85KG

G	Hamza Yerlikaya	TUR
S	Sandor Istvan Bardosi	HUN
B	Mukhran Vakhtangadze	GEO
19	Arek Olczak	AUS

97KG

G	Mikael Ljungberg	SWE
S	David Saldadze	UKR
B	Garrett Lowney	USA
R1	Ben Vincent	AUS

130KG

G	Rulon Gardner	USA
S	Alexandre Kareline	RUS
B	Dmitry Debelka	BLR
18	Laszio Kovaks	AUS

LEGEND

Number next to Australian competitors' names denotes finishing place.

R	Round (Number)
REP	Repechage
DNQ	Did Not Qualify
DNS	Did Not Start
DNC	Did Not Compete
DNF	Did Not Finish
DSQ	Disqualified
QF	Quarter-final
SF	Semi-final

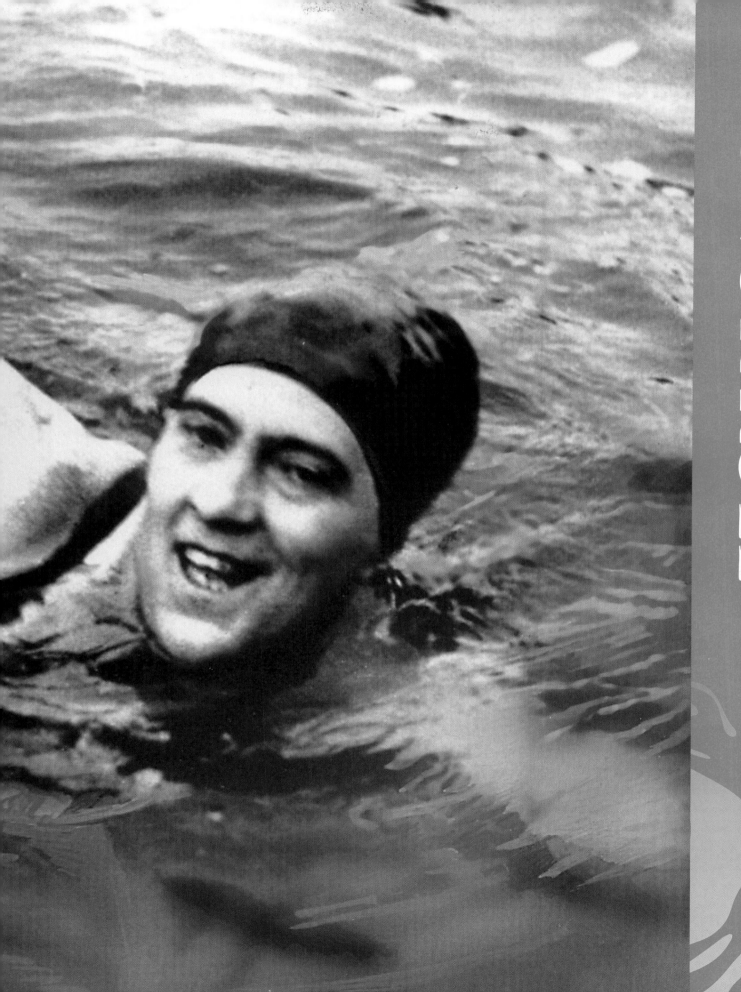

FROM THE BEGINNING

Australia is one of only two nations to have contested each modern Olympiad. Although medals were not awarded until St Louis in 1904, this honor roll acknowledges athletes from the two previous Olympiads as medallists. Here is a complete list of Australian medal winners from 1896 to 1996.

Above: Reginald "Snowy" Baker was a silver medallist as a boxing middleweight in 1908. Right: A stalwart of the Australian swimming team, Frank Beaurepaire won his first Olympic medal in 1908.

Opening spread: Sarah "Fanny" Durack, Australia's first woman gold medallist.

ATHENS 1896

GOLD

Edwin Flack	Track and Field	800m
Edwin Flack	Track and Field	1500m

PARIS 1900

GOLD

Frederick Lane	Swimming	200m freestyle
Frederick Lane	Swimming	200m obstacle
Donald Mackintosh	Shooting	Game shooting

BRONZE

Stanley Rowley	Track and Field	60m
Stanley Rowley	Track and Field	100m
Stanley Rowley	Track and Field	200m
Donald Mackintosh	Shooting	Live pigeon shooting

ST LOUIS 1904

No Australian medal winners, two Australian team members

ATHENS 1906

These Games, where Australia had a team of five, were considered unofficial by the IOC.

SILVER

Harold Healy	Track and Field	110m hurdles

BRONZE

Cecil Healy	Swimming	100m freestyle
Nigel Barker	Track and Field	100m
Nigel Barker	Track and Field	400m

LONDON 1908

GOLD

Rugby Union team	Rugby Union	

SILVER

Reginald "Snowy" Baker	Boxing	Middleweight
Frank Beaurepaire	Swimming	400m freestyle

BRONZE

Frank Beaurepaire	Swimming	1500m freestyle

STOCKHOLM 1912

GOLD

Sarah "Fanny" Durack	Swimming	100m freestyle
Leslie Boardman	Swimming	4x200m freestyle relay
Malcolm Champion (NZ)		
Harold Hardwick		
Cecil Healy		

SILVER

Cecil Healy	Swimming	100m freestyle
Mina Wylie	Swimming	100m freestyle

BRONZE

Harold Hardwick	Swimming	400m freestyle
Harold Hardwick	Swimming	1500m freestyle

ANTWERP 1920

SILVER

George Parker	Track and Field	3000m walk
Frank Beaurepaire	Swimming	4x200m freestyle relay
Harry Hay		
William Herald		
Ivan Stedman		

BRONZE

Frank Beaurepaire	Swimming	1500m freestyle

PARIS 1924

GOLD

Andrew "Boy" Charlton	Swimming	1500m freestyle
Richmond Eve	Diving	Plain high diving
Anthony "Nick" Winter	Track and Field	Hop, Step and Jump

SILVER

Frank Beaurepaire	Swimming	4x200m freestyle relay
Andrew "Boy" Charlton		
Moss Christine		
Ernest Henry		

BRONZE

Frank Beaurepaire	Swimming	1500m freestyle
Andrew "Boy" Charlton	Swimming	400m freestyle

AMSTERDAM 1928

GOLD

Bobby Pearce	Rowing	Single sculls

SILVER

Andrew "Boy" Charlton	Swimming	400m freestyle
Andrew "Boy" Charlton	Swimming	1500m freestyle

BRONZE

Edgar "Dunc" Gray	Cycling	1000m time trial

Left: The pin-up idol of a generation, Andrew "Boy" Charlton.
Right: Richmond "Dick" Eve won gold in the plain high diving at Paris in 1924.

LOS ANGELES 1932

GOLD

Clare Dennis	Swimming	200m breaststroke
Edgar "Dunc" Gray	Cycling	1000m time trial
Bobby Pearce	Rowing	Single sculls

SILVER

Bonnie Mealing	Swimming	100m backstroke

BRONZE

Eddie Scarf	Wrestling	Light-heavyweight

BERLIN 1936

BRONZE

Jack Metcalfe	Track and Field	Hop, Step and Jump

LONDON 1948

GOLD

John Winter	Track and Field	High jump
Merv Wood	Rowing	Single sculls

SILVER

George Avery	Track and Field	Hop, Step and Jump
Theo Bruce	Track and Field	Long jump

Dick Garrand	Wrestling	Welterweight
Nancy Lyons	Swimming	200m breaststroke
John Marshall	Swimming	1500m freestyle
Joyce King	Track and Field	4x100m relay
June Maston		
Betty McKinnon		
Shirley Strickland		

BRONZE

Jim Armstrong	Wrestling	Heavyweight
Judy Joy Davies	Swimming	100m backstroke
John Marshall	Swimming	400m freestyle
Shirley Strickland	Track and Field	100m
Shirley Strickland	Track and Field	80m hurdles

HELSINKI 1952

GOLD

John Davies	Swimming	200m breaststroke
Marjorie Jackson	Track and Field	100m
Marjorie Jackson	Track and Field	200m
Russell Mockridge	Cycling	1000m sprint
Russell Mockridge, Lionel Cox	Cycling	2000m tandem
Shirley Strickland	Track and Field	80m hurdles

Left: The Opening Ceremony of the Berlin Olympic Games in 1936.

Above left: Merv Wood was a gold medallist in rowing at London in 1948, the first Olympic Games after WWII.

Above: Edgar "Dunc" Gray has been immortalised in the name of Sydney's new Olympic velodrome. He won gold in cycling in Los Angeles, 1932.

SILVER

Lionel Cox	Cycling	1000m sprint
Merv Wood	Rowing	Single sculls

BRONZE

Shirley Strickland	Track and Field	100m
Vern Barberis	Weightlifting	Lightweight
Men's Eights	Rowing	

MELBOURNE 1956

GOLD

Betty Cuthbert	Track and Field	100m
Betty Cuthbert	Track and Field	200m
Shirley Strickland	Track and Field	80m hurdles
Betty Cuthbert	Track and Field	4x100m relay
Norma Croker		
Fleur Mellor		
Shirley Strickland		
Lorraine Crapp	Swimming	400m freestyle
Dawn Fraser	Swimming	100m freestyle
Jon Henricks	Swimming	100m freestyle
Murray Rose	Swimming	400m freestyle
Murray Rose	Swimming	1500m freestyle
David Theile	Swimming	100m breaststroke
Lorraine Crapp	Swimming	4x100m freestyle relay
Dawn Fraser		
Faith Leech		
Sandra Morgan		
John Devitt	Swimming	4x200m freestyle relay
Jon Henricks		
Kevin O'Halloran		
Murray Rose		
Ian Browne	Cycling	2000m tandem
Tony Marchant		

SILVER

Graham Gipson	Track and Field	4x400m relay
Kevan Gosper		
Leon Gregory		
David Lean		
Lorraine Crapp	Swimming	100m freestyle

Top left: Shirley Strickland was unbeatable in 80m hurdles at Helsinki, 1952.

Left: The queen of the Melbourne 1956 swimming pool, the incomparable Dawn Fraser.

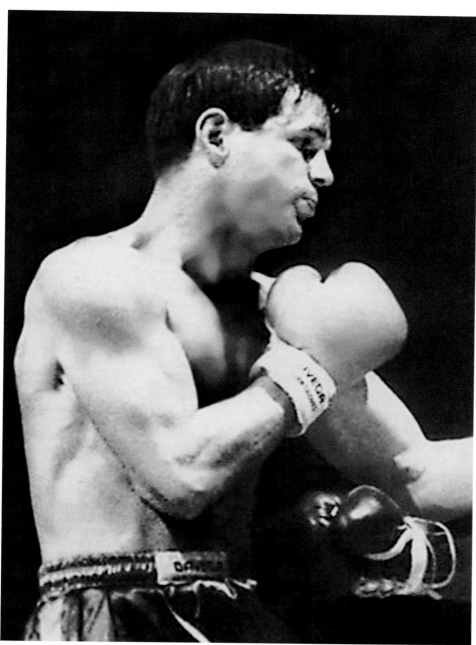

Left: Tony Madigan's opponents in 1960 at Tokyo included a young boxer called Cassius Clay, later Muhammad Ali.

Douglass Buxton	Yachting	5.5 metre class
Jock Sturrock		
Devereaux Mytton		
Warwick Brown	Canoeing	10,000m kayak pairs
Dennis Green		

ROME 1960

GOLD

John Devitt	Swimming	100m freestyle
Herb Elliott	Track and Field	1500m
Dawn Fraser	Swimming	100m freestyle
John Konrads	Swimming	1500m freestyle
Lawrence Morgan	Equestrian	Individual 3 day event
David Thiele	Swimming	100m backstroke
Lawrence Morgan	Equestrian	Team 3 day event
William Roycroft		
Neale Lavis		
Murray Rose	Swimming	400m freestyle

SILVER

Noel Freeman	Track and Field	20km walk
Neville Hayes	Swimming	200m butterfly
Brenda Jones	Track and Field	800m
Neale Lavis	Equestrian	Individual 3 day event
Murray Rose	Swimming	1500m freestyle
David Thiele	Swimming	4x100m medley relay
Terry Gathercole		
Neville Hayes		
Geoff Shipton		
Dawn Fraser	Swimming	4x100m freestyle relay
Ilsa Konrads,		
Lorraine Crapp		
Alva Colquhoun		
Marilyn Wilson	Swimming	4x100m medley relay
Rosemary Lassig		
Jan Andrews		
Dawn Fraser		

BRONZE

Jan Andrew	Swimming	100m butterfly
John Konrads	Swimming	400m freestyle
Tony Madigan	Boxing	Light-heavyweight
Dave Power	Track and Field	10,000m

John Devitt	Swimming	100m freestyle
Dawn Fraser	Swimming	400m freestyle
Stuart McKenzie	Rowing	Single sculls
John Monckton	Swimming	100m backstroke
Charles Porter	Track and Field	High jump
John Scott	Yachting	12 metre class
Roland Tasker		

BRONZE

Gary Chapman	Swimming	100m freestyle
Hector Hogan	Track and Field	100m

Kevin Hogarth	Boxing	Welterweight
John Landy	Track and Field	1500m
Alan Lawrence	Track and Field	10,000m
Faith Leech	Swimming	100m freestyle
Marlene Matthews	Track and Field	100m
Marlene Matthews	Track and Field	200m
Dick Ploog	Cycling	1000m sprint
Norma Thrower	Track and Field	80m hurdles
Murray Riley	Rowing	Double sculls
Merv Wood		
Men's Eights	Rowing	

Above: Shane Gould had one glorious Olympic Games – Munich, 1972.

Opposite: The black power salute at Mexico's Games of 1968, during the 200m medal ceremony with Australia's Peter Norman taking the silver.

Ollie Taylor	Boxing	Bantamweight
John Devitt	Swimming	4x200m freestyle relay
David Dickson		
John Konrads		
Murray Rose		

TOKYO 1964

GOLD

Kevin Berry	Swimming	200m butterfly
Betty Cuthbert	Track and Field	400m
Dawn Fraser	Swimming	100m freestyle
Ian O'Brien	Swimming	200m breaststroke
Robert Windle	Swimming	1500m freestyle
Bill Northam	Yachting	5.5 metre class
Peter O'Donnell		
James Sargeant		

SILVER

Michelle Brown	Track and Field	High jump
Lynette Bell	Swimming	4x100m freestyle relay
Dawn Fraser		
Janice Murphy		
Robyn Thorn		

BRONZE

Judy Amoore	Track and Field	400m
Marilyn Black	Track and Field	200m
Theodore Boronovoksis	Judo	All weight
Ron Clarke	Track and Field	10,000m
Pam Kilborn	Track and Field	80m hurdles
Allan Wood	Swimming	400m freestyle
Allan Wood	Swimming	1500m freestyle
Men's Hockey Team	Field Hockey	
David Dickson	Swimming	4x100m freestyle relay
John Ryan		
Peter Doak		
Robert Windle		
Peter Reynolds	Swimming	4x100m medley relay
Ian O'Brien		
Kevin Berry		
David Dickson		

MEXICO CITY 1968

GOLD

Maureen Caird	Track and Field	80m hurdles
Ralph Doubell	Track and Field	800m
Lyn McClements	Swimming	100m butterfly
Michael Wenden	Swimming	100m freestyle
Michael Wenden	Swimming	200m freestyle

SILVER

Raelene Boyle	Track and Field	200m
Pam Kilborn	Track and Field	80m hurdles
Peter Norman	Track and Field	200m
Men's Hockey Team	Field Hockey	
Men's Eights	Rowing	
Greg Rogers	Swimming	4x200m freestyle relay
Michael Wenden		
Graham White		
Robert Windle		
Lyn McClements	Swimming	4x100m medley relay
Judy Playfair		
Janet Steinbeck		
Lynette Watson		

BRONZE

Greg Brough	Swimming	1500m freestyle
Jenny Lamy	Track and Field	200m
Karen Moras	Swimming	400m
Brian Cobcroft	Equestrian	Team three day event
Wayne Roycroft		
Bill Roycroft		
Robert Cusack	Swimming	4x100m freestyle relay
Greg Rogers		
Michael Wenden		
Robert Windle		

MUNICH 1972

GOLD

Brad Cooper	Swimming	400m freestyle
Shane Gould	Swimming	200m freestyle
Shane Gould	Swimming	400m freestyle
Shane Gould	Swimming	200m individual medley
Gail Neall	Swimming	400m individual medley
Beverley Whitfield	Swimming	200m breaststroke
David Forbes	Yachting	Star class
John Anderson		
John Cuneo	Yachting	Dragon class
Thomas Anderson		
John Shaw		

Top: John Bertrand won silver at Montreal in the Finn class.

Above: The halcyon days of Australian women's distance swimming, Michelle Ford won gold at Moscow in 1980.

Opposite: The herculean Dean Lukin, taking gold in weightlifting, Los Angeles 1984.

SILVER

Raelene Boyle	Track and Field	100m
Raelene Boyle	Track and Field	200m
Danny Clark	Cycling	1000m time trial
Shane Gould	Swimming	800m freestyle
John Nicholson	Cycling	1000m sprint
Kevin "Clyde" Sefton	Cycling	Individual road race
Graham Windeatt	Swimming	1500m freestyle

BRONZE

Shane Gould	Swimming	100m freestyle
Beverley Whitfield	Swimming	100m breaststroke

MONTREAL 1976

SILVER

Men's Hockey Team	Field Hockey	

BRONZE

Stephen Holland	Swimming	1500m freestyle
Mervyn Bennett	Equestrian	Team 3 day event
Denis Piggot		
Wayne Roycroft		
Bill Roycroft		

Ian Brown	Yachting	470 class
Ian Ruff		
John Bertrand	Yachting	Finn class

MOSCOW 1980

GOLD

Michelle Ford	Swimming	800m freestyle
Neil Brooks	Swimming	4x100m medley relay
Peter Evans		
Mark Kerry		
Mark Tonelli		

SILVER

Rick Mitchell	Track and Field	400m
John Sumegi	Canoeing	500m kayak singles

BRONZE

Graeme Brewer	Swimming	200m freestyle
Peter Evans	Swimming	100m breaststroke
Michelle Ford	Swimming	200m butterfly
Mark Kerry	Swimming	200m backstroke
Max Metzker	Swimming	1500m freestyle

LOS ANGELES 1984

GOLD

Dean Lukin	Weightlifting	Super heavyweight
Glynis Nunn	Track and Field	Heptathlon
Jon Sieben	Swimming	200m butterfly
Michael Grenda	Cycling	4000m team pursuit
Kevin Nichols		
Michael Turtur		
Dean Woods		

SILVER

Glenn Beringen	Swimming	200m breaststroke
Gary Honey	Track and Field	Long jump
Robert Kabbas	Weightlifting	Light heavyweight
Suzanne Landells	Swimming	400m individual medley
Karen Phillips	Swimming	200m butterfly
Mark Stockwell	Swimming	100m freestyle
Neil Brooks	Swimming	4x100m medley relay
Michael Delany		
Greg Fasala		
Mark Stockwell		
Gary Gullock	Rowing	Quadruple sculls
Anthony Lovrich		
Timothy McLaren		
Paul Reedy		

BRONZE

Glen Buchanan	Swimming	100m butterfly
Patricia Dench	Shooting	Women's Pistol
Peter Evans	Swimming	100m breaststroke
Justin Lemberg	Swimming	400m freestyle
Gael Martin	Track and Field	Shot put
Michelle Pearson	Swimming	200m individual medley
Rob Woodhouse	Swimming	400m individual medley
Barry Kelly,	Canoeing	1000m K2
Grant Kenny		
Karen Brancourt	Rowing	Women's coxed fours
Susan Chapman		
Margot Foster		
Robin Gray-Gardner		
Susan Lee		
Men's Eights	Rowing	
Glen Buchanan	Swimming	4x100m medley relay
Peter Evans		
Mark Kerry		
Mark Stockwell		

Scott Anderson	Yachting	Tornado class
Christopher Cairns		

SEOUL 1988

GOLD

Duncan Armstrong	Swimming	200m freestyle
Debbie Flintoff-King	Track and Field	400m hurdles
Women's Hockey Team	Field Hockey	

SILVER

Duncan Armstrong	Swimming	400m freestyle
Graham Cheney	Boxing	Light-welterweight
Grant Davies	Canoeing	1000m K1
Lisa Martin	Track and Field	Marathon
Martin Vinnicombe	Cycling	1000m time trial
Dean Woods	Cycling	4000m individual pursuit

Top: Golden reasons to celebrate for Duncan Armstrong in the pool at Seoul.
Above: A legend is made. Kieren Perkins celebrates his first 1500m gold at Barcelona in 1992.

Opposite page, top: Another awesome foursome. Australia's Equestrian Three Day Event team gold medallists on the dais at Atlanta.

BRONZE

Peter Foster	Canoeing	1000m Kayak pairs
Kelvin Graham		
Julie McDonald	Swimming	800m freestyle
Gary Neiwand	Cycling	1000m sprint
Liz Smylie	Tennis	Doubles
Wendy Turnbull		
Brett Dutton	Cycling	4000m team pursuit
Wayne McCarney		
Stephen McGlede		
Dean Woods		

BARCELONA 1992

GOLD

Kieren Perkins	Swimming	1500m freestyle
Clint Robinson	Canoeing	1000m K1
Matthew Ryan	Equestrian	Individual 3 day event
Kathy Watt	Cycling	Individual road race
Andrew Hoy	Equestrian	Team 3 day event
Gillian Rolton		
Matthew Ryan		
Peter Antonie	Rowing	Double sculls
Stephen Hawkins		
Andrew Cooper	Rowing	Coxless Fours
Nick Green		
Mike McKay		
James Tomkins		

SILVER

Glen Housman	Swimming	1500m freestyle
Shane Kelly	Cycling	1000m time trial
Hayley Lewis	Swimming	800m freestyle
Kieren Perkins	Swimming	400m freestyle
Gary Neiwand	Cycling	1000m sprint
Kathy Watt	Cycling	3000m individual pursuit
Danielle Woodward	Canoeing	Slalom
Brett Aitken	Cycling	4000m team pursuit
Steve McGlede		
Shaun O'Brien		
Stuart O'Grady		
Men's Hockey Team	Field Hockey	

BRONZE

Daniela Costian	Track and Field	Discus
Tim Forsyth	Track and Field	High jump
Lars Kleppich	Yachting	Sailboard
Hayley Lewis	Swimming	400m freestyle

Susan O'Neill	Swimming	200m butterfly
Samantha Riley	Swimming	100m breaststroke
Phil Rogers	Swimming	100m breaststroke
Nicole Stevenson	Swimming	200m backstroke
Mitch Booth	Yachting	Tornado class
John Forbes		
Rachel McQuillan	Tennis	Doubles
Nicole Provis		
Ramon Andersson	Canoeing	1000m K4
Kelvin Graham		
Ian Rowling		
Steve Wood		

ATLANTA 1996

GOLD

Australia	Equestrian	Team 3 day event
Michael Diamond	Shooting	Men's Trap
Russell Mark	Shooting	Men's Double Trap
Susan O'Neill	Swimming	200m butterfly
Kieren Perkins	Swimming	1500m freestyle
Megan Still	Rowing	Coxless pairs
Kate Slatter		
Mike McKay	Rowing	Coxless fours
James Tomkins		
Nick Green		
Drew Ginn		
Mark Woodforde	Tennis	Doubles
Todd Woodbridge		

SILVER

Mitch Booth	Yachting	Tornado class
Andrew Landenberger		
Sarah Ryan	Swimming	4x100m medley relay
Susan O'Neill		
Samantha Riley		
Nicole Stevenson		
Angela Kennedy		
Helen Denman		
Michelle Ferris	Cycling	Sprint
Cathy Freeman	Track and Field	400m
Daniel Kowalski	Swimming	1500m freestyle
Louise McPaul	Track and Field	Javelin
Scott Miller	Swimming	100m butterfly
Petria Thomas	Swimming	200m butterfly
David Weightman	Rowing	Coxless pairs
Robert Scott		
Women's Hockey Team	Field Hockey	

BRONZE

Colin Beashel	Yachting	Star class
David Giles		
Stefan Botev	Weightlifting	Super heavyweight
Daniel Collins	Canoeing	500m K2
Andrew Trim		
Anthony Edwards	Rowing	Lightweight double sculls
Bruce Hick		
Scott Goodman	Swimming	200m butterfly
Deserie Huddleston	Shooting	Women's double trap
Rebecca Joyce	Rowing	Lightweight double sculls
Virginia Lee		

Daniel Kowalski	Swimming	200m freestyle
Daniel Kowalski	Swimming	400m freestyle
Brad McGee	Cycling	4000m individual pursuit
Men's Hockey Team	Field Hockey	
Nicole Stevenson	Swimming	4x200m freestyle relay
Susan O'Neill		
Lise Mackie		
Emma Johnson		
Julia Greville		
Brett Aitken	Cycling	Team pursuit
Brad McGee		
Stuart O'Grady		

Tim O'Shannessey		
Dean Woods		
Women's Softball Team	Softball	
Stuart O'Grady	Cycling	40km points race
Kerri Pottharst	Volleyball	Beach volleyball
Natalie Cook		
Samantha Riley	Swimming	100m breaststroke
Clint Robinson	Canoeing	1000m K1
Lucy Tyler-Sharman	Cycling	24km points race
Anna Wood,	Canoeing	500m K2
Katrin Borchert		
Women's Basketball	Basketball	

'IN THE NAME OF ALL
COMPETITORS I PROMISE THAT
WE SHALL TAKE PART IN THESE
OLYMPIC GAMES, RESPECTING AND
ABIDING BY THE RULES WHICH
GOVERN THEM, IN THE TRUE
SPIRIT OF SPORTSMANSHIP, FOR
THE GLORY OF SPORT AND
THE HONOR OF OUR TEAMS'
OLYMPIC OATH

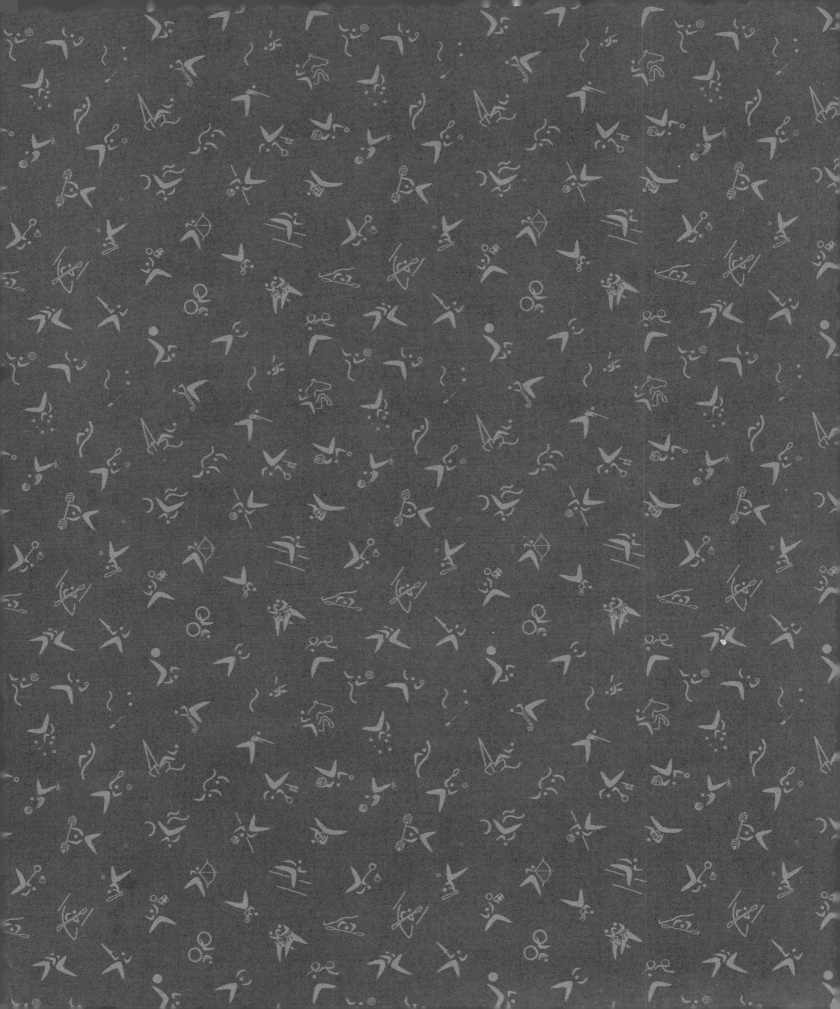